The S*ubstance of* F*ire*

AND OTHER PLAYS

The
Substance of
Fire

AND OTHER PLAYS

Jon Robin Baitz

Theatre Communications Group   New York   1993

Contents

Preface

There's nothing worse than a testimonial dinner speaker who rises to his feet, clears his throat and begins with those chillingly familiar words, "I first met so-and-so when." The story that follows is usually never about so-and-so and always about the speaker and how smart and farsighted he was to have recognized so-and-so's great talent way back when.

But this brief introduction to the plays of Jon Robin Baitz is not so much meant to honor the author as it is to discuss three plays that years from now will be seen as very early efforts in a long and distinguished theatrical career. So please forgive me, and allow me to rise and clear my throat.

I first met Robbie Baitz in the offices of Playwrights Horizons. I had read *The Film Society*, admired it, but had not wanted to produce it because I felt that it would be impossible to cast, and that the author, judging by his play, had to be an elderly protegé of Terrence Rattigan who had undoubtedly spent a lifetime waiting for this one big moment. This was not for youthful, pioneering Playwrights Horizons! I did agree to meet Mr. Baitz and take him to lunch, but only because his agent, the brilliant and terrifying George Lane at William Morris, insisted. I strolled out into the lobby to greet my guest, looking forward to a quick meal and a civilized chat about lemon curd, London traffic and the glory days of Binkie Beaumont. I was stunned. Instead of a seedy old gentleman in a tan raincoat I saw a handsome young man in hip sunglasses and a leather jacket who was not only American but from Los Angeles!

I tell this story to make a point: the three plays in this volume are fascinating because they seem to be the work of someone who is old, who has *lived*, who has a fundamental respect for old-fashioned, civilized, cultivated values. At the same time they seem to be the work of a very young man. They are bold, stylistically audacious, occasionally disheveled and out to dazzle. People used to say after seeing *The Substance of Fire*, "How can someone twenty-eight years old know so much?" And after *The End of the Day* one would hear, "How can someone so young be so cynical?"

A writer listens, a writer observes. And we forget sometimes about talent. Robbie Baitz's combination of youthful impetuousness in the service of a mature, sophisticated world view *is* his talent. His stories are told in graceful, measured, always literate ways. And there's more than a dash of naughty boy wit and incisive verbal bravura. If Arthur Miller had married Noel Coward, their son would have been Robbie Baitz. It's lucky, too, that he has inherited the best qualities of those two great writers and has avoided some of their less attractive traits.

The plays you are about to read are often hilarious, but they are about something deadly serious: the decline and decay of a crumbling world order. In all three plays the leading character fights against or succumbs to the corruption around him. In *The Film Society* a sensitive and potentially progressive young teacher betrays his closest friends in order to achieve power and be made headmaster of the school. In *The Substance of Fire* Isaac Geldhart refuses to accept the economic realities of his struggling publishing house and allows himself to be betrayed by his family and fired from his job rather than publish popular trash. And Graydon Massey, in *The End of the Day*, attracted by American wealth and vulgarity and repulsed by the carelessness and stupidity he sees around him, decides towards the end of the play to join in the fun: The corruption is all over the world, not just in America, so why not cash in?

Robbie Baitz is writing about civilization and its many layers. His plays clearly come from observed life as well as the fertile unconscious from which every good writer draws. And so his *writing* has many layers. Consider the use of fire imagery in *The Substance of Fire*. Or the resonance of the Stubbs painting in *The End of the Day*. And to go to something less literary and more theatrical: consider those favorite old American dramatic themes—parents and the rebellion against parental authority—that are at the heart of each play. Never in recent years has that conflict been so succinctly and appealingly dramatized. As much as we may disapprove of Isaac Geldhart's cruelty to his children in *The*

Substance of Fire, for example, we admire him because he is morally correct and verbally dexterous; we pity him because he is emotionally full and unable to communicate the love he feels.

Before the first preview of *The Substance of Fire* at Playwrights Horizons I remember wondering how the audience would take to such a dense and verbal play. Would they be willing, in this era of limited attention spans and sound bites, to listen and let the language lead them on? I needn't have worried. Those early audiences took to the play with the intensity of parched and desperate beasts gulping down water in the desert. They *wanted* to listen; they *luxuriated* in all those lovely words.

This gave me great hope for the theatre and for the future of a theatre of language. And we have Jon Robin Baitz and a *very* few others to thank for that.

André Bishop
Lincoln Center Theater
September, 1992

The Film Society

To Ulu Grosbard

The Film Society was originally produced in English by The Los Angeles Actors' Theatre/Los Angeles Theatre Center, Bill Bushnell, Artistic Producing Director.

Original New York Production by the Second Stage Theatre, July, 1988.

Characters

JONATHON BALTON
NAN SINCLAIR
TERRY SINCLAIR
NEVILLE SUTTER
MRS. BALTON
HAMISH FOX

Time

Act One
September, 1970.

Act Two
December, 1970

Place

Durban, Natal Province, South Africa.

"The consciences of the English are unnaturally agitated by Africa."
Evelyn Waugh
A Tourist in Africa, 1959.

The Film Society

ACT ONE

Scene One

Jonathon's classroom. Jonathon sits in the dark, watching the last moments of Touch of Evil.

MAN *(V.O.):* "Well. Hank was a great detective all right."
WOMAN *(V.O.):* "And a lousy cop."

(The door is flung open and Hamish Fox enters.)

FOX: What the bloody hell is going on in here! Turn on the lights!
BALTON *(Turning off the projector):* Just watching a film, is all, Hamish!

(He turns on the lights.)

FOX: What do you mean "watching a film"? Where are they?
BALTON: The boys? They didn't—it's not really film society now, I was just watching it again, you see.
FOX: Not the boys! Nan and Terry Sinclair!
BALTON: Not here. I don't know, really, with all the fuss and all, when it was over, I just came in here, you see, and—
FOX: You have anything to do with this fiasco, Balton?
BALTON: Really, I was . . . no! I was in charge of the iced tea, I didn't have anything to do with it.
FOX: Well, they're your friends! You're always giggling together, it's always no good from you lot!
BALTON: No! That's not fair, is it?

FOX: Why're you sitting about in the dark watching a film at a time like this, when we've got policemen all over the place, hey?

BALTON: I don't know why it's such a bother, it's not like we were invaded, Hamish. Terry brought up one African speaker, I don't see why you had to call the entire Durban military out.

(Pause.)

FOX *(staring incredulously at Jonathon):* That's very good! You defend them then and we'll see what happens when we're overrun! This is not some commie summer camp! It's Blenheim! The nerve! Bloody outrageous!

BALTON: I had nothing to do with it, don't shout at me!

(Neville Sutter enters.)

SUTTER: Any sign of the Sinclairs?

FOX: They're hiding.

SUTTER: Calm down, Hammy.

FOX: Don't tell me to calm down. There's been a lot of lefty nonsense going on here lately . . .

SUTTER: Jonathon, I expect you didn't have anything to do with this business, did you? I've just spent the past hour with a roomful of angry parents and it's an awful bore.

BALTON: No, I didn't at all! Because, you see, I had iced tea and meringues and all to organize for after the speeches and prizes and then, in all the fuss and all, I just came back here because, you see, I had ordered *Touch of Mink,* but they sent *Touch of Evil* . . . which I quite liked.

SUTTER:—Jonathon, it's all right, you needn't—

BALTON:—and I wanted to see it again, because the boys didn't quite get it.

FOX: Stop going on about your film society this second!

BALTON: It was all about Mexicans and corruption.

SUTTER *(Sighing):* Jonathon, if any of the parents come looking for me, or the Sinclairs for that matter—

FOX:—Not bloody likely. They're retreating to Moscow—

SUTTER: Tell the Sinclairs, I want to see them up at my house. Joyce tripped over a chair during the commotion. *(He starts to exit)* Come along, Hammy, we'd better finish up with the parents.

FOX *(Following Sutter):* I told you not to put Sinclair in charge of Centenary Day, but you refused to listen, well, all I can say is . . .

SUTTER *(To Fox, off):* Tell the girl to bring the parents a drink in my office and some ice for Joyce's leg, would you? There's a good chap.

(Pause. Balton sighs. Looks outside after them. Turns off the lights, turns on the projector, and watches the remaining moments of the film.)

MAN: "Is that all you have to say for him?"

(Pianola theme on soundtrack.)

WOMAN: "He was some kind of man. What does it matter what you say about people?"

MAN: "Goodbye, Tanya."

WOMAN: "Adios."

(Pianola theme on soundtrack. The door opens. Nan enters as the film credits begin.)

NAN: Jonathon? Jonathon? Where's Terry?

BALTON: Get in here! They're looking all over for you and they're mad as hornets!

NAN: Terry's not here? God, he just disappeared.

BALTON: He went down to Durban jail to see if he could bail out that black priest you two brought up to the podium.

NAN: Me? Christ, I had nothing to do with it! You think I'd allow a stupid gesture like that? He got this man arrested! I had nothing to do with it!

BALTON: You'll have to tell Neville and Hamish that and then it'll all die down, I'm sure. If you explain that . . . as for Terry, well. My. My. You know?

NAN: Jonathon, he's done us in! They're going to sack us this time! It's over.

BALTON: No they won't! Just tell them how terribly sorry

you both are and start to cry for a bit and it'll all be fine. Just like all the other little—episodes.

NAN: He's been so furtive, like one of the boys, I knew something was up! Damn it!

BALTON: I have a bit of whisky, you know!

NAN: Oh hell, sure.

(Jonathon takes two teacups and a bottle of Scotch out of his desk, pours.)

BALTON: Yes, this'll calm you down. I was quite rattled by the whole business myself, I must admit. But it'll all blow over, don't you worry. Storm in a tea-thingie, eh?

NAN: But you know what this town is like! If they fire us, we'll be dead as cold mutton! I can't stand it anymore, he lies, goes off to these ludicrous little meetings, comes back with new words and books and it's all so childish.

BALTON: You'd have thought he'd have learnt his lesson after the parents went mad when he brought in those colored hippie fellows with the guitars and the big hair. My God.

(Terry enters, smiling.)

TERRY: Well. Quite a day, eh?

NAN: Terry, you are an idiot!

TERRY: No! I know exactly what I'm doing. Give me a drink.

BALTON *(Pouring whisky for Terry):* They're quite upset, I think, actually. They want you up at Neville's house, 'cause you somehow managed to trip his wife when you brought that native up. But I wouldn't go for a bit, I'd let it all die down.

NAN: What happened to that man you brought up? Who is he? They dragged him off . . .

TERRY: Reverend Elias Bazewo, and he's been arrested before, I followed him down there—they'll let him go tonight—it's nothing, it's happened before to him, he's fine.

NAN: Don't stand there smiling! How do you think it feels? Being dragged into this?

TERRY: Oh, it's wonderful. Both of you! This place has got to change and we all know it and someone has to do something. They all listened to him! Until Fox called the cops on him—

NAN: They were not listening! They just saw this black man and started screaming, I could have told you what was going to happen.

BALTON: I may not have understood it all, but the general effect was pretty scary. All those pink faces melting in the sun, tea cakes and meringues sticking to their laps. All they asked you to do was put together a nice dull little Centenary Day thingie and it was meant to be nice and sweet and dull, deathly dull hopefully, like last year when they had the choir sing "The Halleluiah Chorus" for six hours straight.

NAN: It's supposed to be a celebration of a hundred years of Blenheim, Terry, that's all!

TERRY: Well, they got one. I can't stand the stagnation anymore. He talked about the blessings of education! Not armed revolution!

NAN: I don't care! If you had told me what you were up to I might feel differently, but it's the childish plotting. You jump on these bandwagons, Terry, without really thinking. Do you think these boys give a damn about politics?

BALTON: It's true, Terry. They only like sports. And besides, you forget what it was like when we were boys here! All forced marches and military history and all that navigating by the stars and gutting wildebeests every morning . . . much better now! Yes it is!

TERRY: How? Both of you are being so narrow-minded. I'm amazed.

NAN: Where do you think you are? University of Natal debate club? This is Blenheim School for Boys!

BALTON: It's true! Let me give you an example of how things're better, as I see it. My film society, for one.

TERRY: Oh, Jonathon, please. The other day you told me that you loved film society because it was a bit of a rest for you. It's not some cultural institution. What'd you show them last week?

BALTON: *Passport to Pimlico*, Terry, see. Perfectly wonderful story and the boys loved it and this week we had *Touch of Evil.*

TERRY: That's not so bad.

BALTON: Actually I had ordered *Touch of Mink,* you see I'm trying to go through it alphabetically . . .

NAN: Terry, I'm sick of it. I'm a schoolteacher, not an activist, and nor are you. It's one thing to have boys over to listen to your new Bob Dylan album and let them smoke on the verandah and to refuse to cane 'em, fine. Treat them like human beings, but not these antagonistic little jabs—you just brought that man here to get attention for yourself.

BALTON: You've always been—when we were boys, Nan, he used to—

TERRY: Are you both honestly so furious at me? *(Pause)* Please don't be angry. Think how it might've been. If instead of calling the police, Hamish Fox had sat there listening. *(He smiles. Goes on calmly)* Elias Bazewo has been teaching black children at a school in Kwamashu for thirty years. He's a man of peace with a great deal of experience and a perspective on education that I thought would remind all of us how privileged we are. How bad would that have been? I guess it wasn't possible.

(Pause.)

NAN: Well, it didn't come off that way, did it? I just don't want to be misled by you. Is that reasonable?

TERRY *(After a moment):* It's just that sometimes you're so clear-headed and practical and pragmatic that we do nothing.

BALTON: Please don't fight.

(Beat.)

TERRY: Perhaps taking action requires a certain amount of stupid faith. I am sorry about not telling you, I don't like keeping things from you.

BALTON: He's sorry, Nan. He didn't mean anything bad to happen, you know that, Nan. It just didn't work out. Like Gilerakis and his pen pal society. Only one boy joined and he ended up sending postcards to his niece in Hong Kong and she never wrote back, so that was a bust . . . *(He smiles)* Not to mention Viltonian.

NAN: Please, Jonathon. Stop it.

BALTON: He had his lizard boys.

TERRY *(Laughing):* It was reptile society and you know it.

BALTON: Right, reptile society, all I know was one little bugger was bitten on the nose and the entire thing packed up, so. Not to mention the horror of "sea shell club." Boys lolling about the beachfront all day. Sutter went mad, I remember. I was one of 'em. Takes a long time for things to work here at Blennies. Maybe if you started a political society . . . ?

TERRY: Jonathon. You miss the point. Why do you always miss the point?

BALTON: I'm just saying it's all getting more reasonable, slowly, if you don't force it. Just apologize to Sutter and Fox and keep it very simple and all in the classroom.

NAN: Jonathon!

BALTON: Yes, Nan! Really. I've yet to open a text book once this year. In history, I just showed them that Michael Caine film where ten men wipe out the entire Zulu army, no one suffers so much as a scratch, everybody gets a Victoria Cross at the end, and the boys're pleased as punch and then you rush 'em all off to see the native dancers, give 'em a bloody great quiz and there you have it. South African history in a nutshell.

TERRY: Look, let's go down to the beachfront, and have some dinner. I'll buy you both dinner and you can shout at me a bit more if you like, and we'll sort it all out like adults, okay? Please?

BALTON *(Beginning to exit):* I can't, I'm sorry. I booked a ticket, you see, it's the last night. I've got to go now so as not to miss the short. They're showing a film at the library. All about an unconventional lady in America and her boy and all the troubles . . . Auntie . . . thingie . . .

TERRY: Auntie thingie? It may be all orchid shows and cricket finals down here at Blennies, but the rest of the world, my boy, is not exactly quiet.

BALTON *(Stopping):* No, it's not. Is it? Well. Look. Don't pro-
voke them. Just let it all die down, will you? Please? I
don't want anything to happen. Politics, Terry. I'm the
last person to talk to about politics. I can't even get a
print of *Touch of Mink.*

(He exits. Nan looks at Terry, sighs.)

NAN: Well, we better think of something to say to Sutter and
Fox.

TERRY: Oh don't worry. They like having me here. To turn
about, to prove utterly wrong. Eh? *(Beat)* Let's go see
'em now.

(Lights down.)

Scene Two

*Jonathon's classroom. The next day. He is at his
desk, wading unhappily through a pile of essays.*

BALTON *(Reading incredulously):* "The Panama Canal . . .
links . . . Africa and America . . ."? God. *God.* How do
they get into this school? *(He reaches into his desk,
takes out a cigar, unwraps and cuts, but does not light
it. Puts it in his mouth. Sighing and thinking. Then, he
writes):* "Cleasby. Uh. . . . Don't you know this is 1970?
Look at the world a bit more closely, thank you. Pass.
But watch it."Odd.

*(Jonathon looks up at the ceiling, notices some-
thing and stands on top of the desk. He does not
see Neville Sutter enter.)*

Very odd.
SUTTER: Jonathon?
BALTON: Neville!
SUTTER: Here late, aren't you?
BALTON: So're you!
SUTTER: Yes, but I live here, don't I?

BALTON: Well, there you are. Rather lot of dust up here. Looks like one of those sea thingies.

SUTTER: Jonathon, get down at once, you're giving me vertigo.

BALTON: I think I shall teach from here from now on. It's rather majestic.

SUTTER: Terribly cold for September.

BALTON: Oh but warm in here, isn't it?

SUTTER: Better in than out.

BALTON: They say—I read somewhere—there's something tricky going on with the polar ice-thingies.

SUTTER: Yes. They're melting. Be underwater any day now. Ice caps and penguins.

BALTON: Was just thinking. Don't like the school uniform.

SUTTER: Perfectly fine uniform.

BALTON: Oh no it's not. In fact, when I was a boy, I asked you why we didn't have long trousers. "This is Africa. Got to be tough."

SUTTER: Excuse me?

BALTON: Your reply. I said, "Well, it's cold here, sir, long trousers would be much better." And that was your answer. "Africa. Gotta be tough." Do you still think so? 'Cause, you know, when I'm asked the same question, know what I say?

SUTTER: Africa gotta be tough?

BALTON: No, no, no. I say, "Headmaster Sutter feels, this being Africa and all, you boys best toughen yourselves up!" And they laugh like hell, you know, 'cause they're pretty fuckin' tough already, these little shits.

SUTTER: Oh please. Let's not be gutter. I'm not in the mood.

BALTON: I'm sorry, it's just that when one is with children all day and then an adult happens to wander in, it makes one a bit giddy.

SUTTER: Yes, I know. Confiscated a yo-yo yesterday and found myself playing with it for hours. So. Did you have your film society today?

BALTON (Instantly suspicious): Why're you asking?

SUTTER: What'd you mean "why"? I'm headmaster—take an interest in the various projects going on.

BALTON (*Scornful*): Right. Like reptile society and sea shell club?

SUTTER: Oh don't remind me. Well? Did you?

BALTON: Actually, no. And I'm quite upset. McNally just forced—literally marched in here and took them off on some sort of arsonists' training decathlon or twenty mile marathon, I mean—came right in, Neville! Stole my—*conscripted* my boys! This has never happened before, Nev?

SUTTER: Showing nice films, then?

BALTON: Nice? Yes, had a wonderful program scheduled today. *Top Hats.*

SUTTER: The boys benefit? An exposure to culture?

BALTON: That's my point. Exposure to culture.

SUTTER: Have you shown any travel films?

(Beat.)

BALTON: Tr-*travel* films?

SUTTER: Exactly. Say, Malaysia, Australia, Ohio and Greece?

BALTON: Ohio and *Greece*?

SUTTER: Or—even better really—closer to home; say Cape Town, Kimberly . . . ?

BALTON: Who the hell wants to see bloody Kimberly? I'd have a room full of empty boys—of empty desks, I mean.

SUTTER: I've got a marvelous collection of photographs that Joyce shot on her trips 'round the country.

BALTON: Oh, why not call it "little slide show society"? You said I could have absolute free reign with film society. *(Beat)* This is totally unacceptable, Neville.

SUTTER: I know I did. I know what I *said*.

BALTON: So . . . you . . . you let McNally take my boys.

SUTTER: We have had, thanks to Terry, four boys so far pulling out as of next week. All going to Durban High.

BALTON: Good! Let 'em go. What's it to do with film society?

SUTTER: Plenty. They give us money. We need money. Jonathon. Terry's guest of honor has died of a heart attack in his cell. I got a call from the police. It will be in the newspaper tomorrow.

BALTON: Good God? A heart attack? But . . . why'd they hold him anyway? You'd think they'd just let him go . . . a priest and all. . . . But, Neville. It's hardly our fault, is it?

SUTTER: No, but think of this as one of the shock waves emanating from Centenary Day and you'll have some idea of what I'm saying regarding film society.

BALTON: *(Sitting down):* Wait. I'm utterly lost . . . there's no connection here . . . I had nothing to do with . . . I mean . . . why?

SUTTER: Why? The parents. They've become very suspicious, very frightened—they're forming a parents' committee and when that happens, it's hell. Believe me. Putsches, coups d'etat, purges. You see, moods change. And the parents've been fairly passive until bloody Terry had to turn Centenary Day into a commie fest. Now they think this is some sort of terribly Bohemian institution.

BALTON: Blenheim? Are they mad?

SUTTER: You don't understand. There's to be a New Blenheim. The parents want—total discipline. And no more nonsense.

BALTON: How *dare* they!

SUTTER: And you're going to feel the pinch too.

BALTON: Go on.

SUTTER: Parents are wondering what's going on in the dark here—in the middle of the day, middle of the week. What're these boys watching? What are they doing? That sort of thing.

BALTON: Tell them to take their boys! They can all go to Durban High or hell for that matter. We don't care, do we? Tell them to fuck off! Fuck 'em! Just tell them really to go and fuck themselves, Neville!

SUTTER: I would never be so socially unattractive. We do care is the point. Can't have classrooms without boys.

BALTON: What a bloody marvelous idea. Look, Nev. You admitted, didn't you, that there had to be something besides cricket, rugger and all the drudgery that builds up? The thing that separates Blenheim from Durban High is that our boys come out of here with imagination. We've always encouraged the boys to look out at the world and feel a certain something about their place in it. No? Yes!

SUTTER: I really wish you wouldn't argue with me. I am the headmaster. I know what I'm doing. I do own the school. Remember? Sometimes, I swear to God, it seems everyone forgets.

BALTON: Well, I'll speak to the parents. They know me. I'm a Balton, for Christ's sake. Leave my film society out of your New Blenheim, Neville, all right?

SUTTER: But, my dear boy, this is one of those gruesome periods of readjustment and no compromise, no discipline, means no parents' support, no Blenheim and no film society.

(Beat. Jonathon nods.)

BALTON: It's Terry. I've warned him a million times, he's making it harder for all of us.

(Beat. Sutter nods.)

SUTTER: Yes. Unfortunately.

BALTON: Oh God.

SUTTER: The thing is, we think we're going to have to let them both go, you see.

BALTON: That would be a stupid, stupid mistake! Who runs this place?

SUTTER: Haven't you listened to a word I've told you? Hasn't he brought it upon himself? How many times has he skirted this? The colored folk singers at assembly? The excursion to worker housing at the sugar refinery? Eh? The constant attacks on the government in senior history class?

BALTON: Yes, yes, yes. I know all about it. Little scandals. . . . Look. Shout at the man a bit. I don't know. And Nan? Why must you drag her into this? She had nothing to do with any of it.

SUTTER: They're *married*! How could she not?

BALTON *(Laughing bitterly)*: Well, she didn't. You've known Terry for thirty-some years—is he not a sly man when he wants to be?

SUTTER: Yes! Exactly! That's why he has to go!

BALTON: He's also the only one here with any brains. And as for the ludicrous notion of firing Nan, you and I both know that she's been the best thing for this place. Lively, funny—it's like a morgue in the teacher's lounge without her.

SUTTER: The parents are a bit suspicious of her.

BALTON: Tell them that she has no interest in Terry's political thingies. She indulges him, as we do.

SUTTER: I do honestly hate to let the parents push us about quite so much.

BALTON: That's my point exactly.

(Pause.)

SUTTER: Well, we shall have to see. *(Beat)* Have you glasses?

BALTON: Tea cups, top right. *(Points to desk)*

SUTTER: Yes. One's spirits tend to flag at about half-past six.

BALTON: Blood sugar dropping.

(Sutter hands Jonathon his drink, Sutter taking a drink before speaking.)

SUTTER: How'd you like to be assistant headmaster?

BALTON: What?

SUTTER: Hamish Fox has spinal cancer.

BALTON: Spinal . . . ? How ghastly. I thought it was just the flu. Good God. Oh, poor man. My God.

SUTTER: And on top of that—on top of everything else, my eyes continue to go out on me.

BALTON: Well, there's eyes for you.

SUTTER: So. If you were to pass it up, I'd have to go to McNally, you see.

BALTON: Good Bloody Christ in Heaven!

SUTTER: My point exactly.

BALTON: This place is turning into hell suddenly. What's going on?

SUTTER: No, it's been building, it's just that you've had a quiet time of it until now. You never come to staff meetings, you never listen. You just think it all lurches forward unremarkably. Well, let me tell you, Jonathon,

when you become assistant head, you lose your invisi-
bility. And you find yourself becoming more of the
representative. And you've got to acknowledge what it
is you're representing. Fox, McNally, parents' commit-
tees, rugger teams, marching boys, all of it. Understand?

(Pause.)

BALTON: What you're saying is . . . "Time for a change." Eh?
SUTTER: Precisely.
BALTON: Assistant head, eh? Well. Then McNally would
leave me alone . . . and . . . Mother'd be pleased. Finally.
About something. Look. I'll tell you what. If we must
have a change, how'd it be if I showed a travel short
once a week?
SUTTER: A harmless exposure to culture that the parents will
appreciate. A film on monkeys. On photosynthesis and
pollination, that sort of thing.
BALTON: Alright, but leave Nan alone and tell McNally to
keep away from my boys. They're not all marathonists.
SUTTER: Agreed. Good. See how we can circumvent the problems if we work together? Exactly. I'm exhausted.
Well, how 'bout a little toast?
BALTON: Smashing.
SUTTER: Er. Let's see. A toast . . . to . . .

*(Both men stand still for a moment, Jonathon
watching Neville attentively. Finally, Neville
merely shrugs and downs his drink. Jonathon follows suit, as lights fade.)*

Scene Three

*Nan and Terry's flat. Early evening. They both
enter. He has on a dark suit, she a dark dress.*

TERRY *(Quietly):* Do you want a drink, love?
NAN: Yes, please, I . . .

(She sits down, rubs her eyes.)

TERRY: Do they think we're all morons. People stopped believing fucking "heart attack in his cell" fifteen years ago, at least go for "fell on his head while falling." A bit of imagination. Right—I wonder if Jackson left any supper, did you speak to him before we left?

NAN: No.

(Terry goes off for a moment, returns with a plate of sandwiches, puts them next to Nan.)

TERRY: God bless Jackson and his little cucumber sandwiches.

NAN: Did you see them taking photographs?

TERRY *(Pouring two drinks)*: Yes. It was probably the Bureau of State Security, I imagine. They do that at funerals.

(Pause.)

NAN: Are they—are they going to come here, do you think?

TERRY: I don't think so. They know my family, they'll leave us alone. That's my estimate, at any rate. I don't know, perhaps they're not impressed by old names. They pulled Bazewo off the podium and they killed him and I can't even get bloody arrested. *(Phone rings. Answering)*: Hello, Jonathon? Um, look, sorry I can't talk now, I'll call you back. Goodbye. *(He hangs up. Pause)* I think our phone's bugged.

NAN: How can you tell?

TERRY: Very telling little click. There's some little fuck with a Sony down at police headquarters. I could almost smell their heavy Vortrecker breathing.

NAN: Our bookshelves are filled with banned books, Terry.

TERRY: Yes, I know.

NAN: I think we ought to do something about them.

TERRY: What? Burn them?

NAN: You're surrounded by a lot of misery right now, Terry, and I think you should listen to me. We've just come from a pathetic funeral in the middle of a dusty cemetery in the middle of nowhere, twenty silly people singing "We Shall Overcome," having their pictures snapped by the police, so, perhaps you should burn your books, yes.

TERRY *(Nodding):* Yes. It was a stupid funeral, wasn't it?

NAN: Well, I haven't been to very many happy ones, love, have you?

TERRY: Listen, if you're this angry at me, then please tell me what you want me to say and I'll say it because I'm—

NAN: Angry? Oh, I've been angry for days. I'm tired to death of being angry. Tell me what you intend to do. No more silence. No more sneaking. They fired you, Terry, and Bazewo is dead, so I want to know what you want to do. *(She gets up, looks outside)* God. You should've known. They arrested Julius Baskin the day he graduated from bloody medical school! You saw what they did to him! He's been under house arrest since '67! What? Are you jealous? How many people does he get to save sitting about at home? We're schoolteachers and you're probably going to be unhireable after this.

TERRY: While you were at school this morning, about a dozen parents called to tell me that they admired what I tried to do and they were furious I was sacked.

NAN: Oh God, Terry . . .

TERRY: Not that it matters anymore, I mean, just to fold up like this after twelve years? Especially after this man has died . . .

NAN: No. Whatever you're thinking, it won't work. There's a parents' committee being formed and they're much stronger than the few families that're behind you, Terry. You'll just make it worse.

TERRY: Doesn't it make you sick? Look at this beachfront— little amusement park, rust and booze and sunken garden filled with cops. It's like I said to Bazewo, "Elias, old mate, Blenheim is a broad-minded, reasonable place." Well, I didn't know how wrong I was. You think it was attention-getting on my part, and perhaps it was, but please don't lord over me with your beachfront. Jesus, it's agony.

(Beat.)

NAN: What will end up happening, actually, is very simple. I shall be fired as well, instantly, at the first sign of trouble from you.

TERRY: No you won't. I had calls from the DeVilliers, the Dixons, the Mellons, Templeton, Soltair—the list goes on—incensed that I was fired and offering to call Neville.

NAN: Well, Fox will be very receptive, won't he? I agree that firing you was un—

TERRY: Yes, well, Fox is dying and that's just fine because nobody could be that brutal for so many years without developing a fatal illness. The whole place is in the midst of this phenomenal earthquake and I'm part of it.

NAN: Terry. Listen to yourself.

(Pause.)

TERRY: If they won't have me back and you're left there spinning in the wind, if I cannot get another job here, if it's all so pointless and miserable, then perhaps we should just pack it in and leave.

NAN: Leave.

TERRY: We've talked about it before.

NAN: Idly, Terry. Idly.

TERRY: This is not out of the blue. Are you afraid to leave?

NAN: I'm afraid for you!

TERRY: Oh God, Nan, I'm fine. Please, don't sit there looking at me like that.

NAN: I have parents here. They haven't got a lot of time left, I'm not going to leave them, think about it. Think about me, for a change. Do you think leaving is the answer?

TERRY: I don't know . . .

NAN: *(Almost in tears):* But you—you would—are you saying you would go without me? God, is that it? Is that how—we're—you can't just dictate to me—your terms! I love you. I want to share this with you, what you're in—don't threaten me—please. Please.

(Pause.)

TERRY: I don't know.

NAN: I almost have to laugh. We have . . . what, five hundred rand in the bank. Not exactly a fortune. God, listen to me being practical, I'm gonna die from practical one of these days.

TERRY: Well, I could see my parents at the farm. I'm sure they'd be relieved to give me something to finally see me off, having forsaken a tenth of one of the better sugarcane outfits in Natal.

NAN: Your parents? Terry, you don't even speak to them and you'd take their money. Terry, I . . . am exhausted. We just watched them put a man under and I feel, for my part, somehow responsible. Isn't that odd? I don't want to discuss this anymore tonight, I want another drink in fact, I want a booze-up and a cold shower, and, frankly, a break from you for a few hours.

TERRY: Nan, I see us wasting away here forever. Before we drove to that ridiculous sham of a funeral, I shared Jackson's rice and beans with him and we sat on the verandah. I suggested to him that the beans might be a bit softer and he started to cry. Isn't that something? There we were, about to go off to Bazewo's funeral—and there was Jackson, the only homosexual Zulu servant in all of Durban, weeping over his beans. And it was all suddenly very clear to me—shudderingly clear. You and me, politely wasting away in old khakis with bad teeth, craving new books and new causes, all of us, weighted down effectively forever by this great entropy down here. I just cannot abide the feeling of being utterly defeated and paunchy.

(Pause.)

NAN: Yes, well, in the meantime, would you do something about those books. Because when they come in here with a warrant, none of it will make any sense or matter in the slightest.

TERRY: My passport. It's expired.

(She exits, leaving him standing alone, looking out over the Durban beachfront.)

Scene Four

Lights up on Mrs. Balton's flat which exudes a faded, Edwardian air of decayed elegance. Mrs. B. has on an absurd African kaaftan, is clutching a whisky and a cigarette. She and Jonathon are surrounded by a number of men's suits.

BALTON: Oh look, I know you're excited, but really, I find the entire subject utterly incomprehensible, Mother. Accountants? Might as well be speaking Balinese.

MRS. BALTON: No, it's very simple! You're doing so splendidly, all I'm asking is for you to be the slightest bit attentive when they come by. Listen to what they're saying, engage with them a bit.

BALTON: You've managed fine without me for centuries, darling. I don't understand the problem.

MRS. BALTON: The issue is where all the accounts are and how to keep track of 'em.

BALTON: Then get a secretary-thingie or something, some service that does figures and numbers and all that business.

MRS. BALTON: No, you don't understand. It seems the accounts in Cape Town were transferred to Salisbury for some reason and then London and now they tell me they've found a bit in Zurich, all of which your father never bothered telling anyone about. And I don't want you to muddle about—an assistant head cannot afford to be ignorant of his monies.

BALTON: Not ignorant, Mother. Just not interested and, besides, what's it got to do with being assistant head— they're totally unrelated.

MRS. BALTON: Oh, love. I'm only trying to help. You've realized that survival is not automatic in this life, right?

BALTON: What's not automatic?

MRS. BALTON: Was not the farm a tangled bush of savagery before your father planted sugarcane? And did we not have to burn it back constantly?

BALTON: Yes, I'll say. Snakes and cats and all, quite a business and—

MRS. BALTON *(Cutting him off):* A business, exactly! Just like being involved with the accountants.

BALTON: Well, darling. Wouldn't you say it's useless to talk to me about business at this late date? Just when I've become so busy being assistant head? And may I just say, I mean, really, the way you go on about the farm and the bush, it's as dull as dirty dishwater. We haven't owned it since I was a boy, right? And it's your only frame of reference these days. It's so provincial. I mean, can't we just be adults here?

(Pause. He stares at her knowingly. She stares back.)

MRS. BALTON: All I'm saying is I've bought you these marvelous suits and wouldn't it be nice if you were to take on some corresponding responsibilities? That's the only thing I'm saying. Aren't they lovely?

BALTON: Quite a world. The world of clothes, eh?

MRS. BALTON: And to succeed in your field? A marvel. That's all I'm saying.

BALTON: And then one has one's suits, eh?

MRS. BALTON: Why not try on the yellow?

BALTON *(Beginning to undress):* If you like. You know, just thinking; after we moved to the city from the farm and I went off to Blennies, I was bloody worried 'bout managing, remember? All rashes and coughs, eh? But you know what? It turns out, it doesn't seem to make the slightest bit of difference. I've done fine without the least bit of managing. One worries. One frets. And in the end they go and make you assistant head.

MRS. BALTON: The point is, you're assuming your natural leadership tendencies.

BALTON: But that's the point! I don't have any! You know that! It's a joke!

MRS. BALTON: Well, perhaps you might if you wore better undies. There's a bloody great hole the size of a krugerrand in your backside.

BALTON: Well, nobody ever sees the damn things, Mother, unfortunately. Quite a world. The world of . . . the suit. *(He puts on the yellow linen jacket)* How do I look?

MRS. BALTON: Like your father. An aristocrat in his linen suits! Where's nanny? Where is she? She's got to see this, she won't believe it—you look just like him! Where is she?

(She rings furiously.)

BALTON: Going as deaf as a bat is where she is, love.

MRS. BALTON: I know.

(She rings again.)

BALTON: Well leave her alone. You run her ragged, poor dear, probably in a coma. *(Beat)* I do like the lapel, though.

MRS. BALTON: Oh it's true. Just like Christopher, you look.

BALTON: Well then. I suppose we've made a success of it, eh? *(He stands for a moment)* It's interesting, what a new suit does, isn't it? *(Beat)* I have plans, you know, Mother. I have plans.

MRS. BALTON: Tell me!

BALTON *(Quietly, almost a reverie):* Oh, it's fairly mundane, really, more of a spirit of growth, let people like Gilerakis and his pen pal boys thrive, bring in some more women teachers—you know how stuffy it gets in the faculty lounge, all cigars and sports talk and off-color little jokes. We haven't had a dramatics society since I was a boy. Terry and I did panto at Christmas . . . remember?

MRS. BALTON: Yes, I remember.

BALTON: I feel so old sometimes, Mother. I feel old today. Isn't that odd?

MRS. BALTON: We're all getting on, nanny stumbling about, love, and me, well, look at me . . .

BALTON: You? Nonsense, you'll outlive us all, darling . . . no, I walked in to my classroom today. My classroom. Hah! Who would've thought. It's a pity doing radio drama didn't work out. That was the life I was meant for, that was the life for me. Sitting about, chatting with the other show people, going on about the new styles, the new scripts and all . . . pots of tea and glasses of whisky and cigarettes. There was nothing better, nothing like it. *(Beat)* No use reminiscing, eh? None at all.

MRS. BALTON: Let's have a drink, shall we, love, before dinner?

TERRY *(Entering):* Hello . . . ? You know, I've told you, you can't leave your door wide open anymore. Lots of angry natives milling about these days, eh . . . hello . . .

MRS. BALTON: Hello, Terry, come in, Terry darling.

(He kisses her.)

Sit down. I'm sure you'd know more about all that than we would, eh? Let's give him a drink shall we, Jon-Jon?

TERRY: Not for me, thanks, no, I know you wanted to talk to me.

BALTON: Terry, I'm glad you're here, I was going to call you again. I would like to go with you to your friend's funeral, I think, I . . .

MRS. BALTON: What a sweet idea. How lovely . . .

TERRY *(Seriously):* I'm sorry, Jonathon, but it was yesterday, you see.

MRS. BALTON: Oh dear. What a ghastly time it's been for you, dear.

BALTON: I didn't know. There wasn't a word in the papers.

TERRY: Really, it's all right, it wasn't expected of you. There were plenty of people there. His children had a marvelous time of it.

BALTON: Terry, I know you must be angry at all of us—this whole business.

TERRY: No, I have nothing to be angry at. Is that why you wanted to see me?

BALTON: No, no, no. Please. I know you. I know how you think and I'm sorry, I must ask you, please do not try anything. Not now.

TERRY: Really, Jonathon. I'm done. You needn't worry.

BALTON: Yes, but I'm worried. You must understand, Nan is just barely hanging on. And if you provoked them, if you tried anything, there'd be nothing I could do. Terry. It would be out of my hands, they'd fire her in a shot.

(Beat.)

TERRY *(Nodding. Softening):* Yes. Nan said the same thing.

BALTON: So you understand this?

TERRY: No, quite. *(Beat)* I must rethink everything.

BALTON: If they let her go, there'd be no one left for me. I'd be all alone, those people hardly say a word to me, they never even smile at me. It has just been the three of us and I don't want to . . . endanger Nan. With you gone, I've got to do all of it on my own, I've no support and I don't know what to do.

TERRY: Well . . . it turns out, I seem to have some people on my side.

BALTON: What?

TERRY: . . . Yes. Parents calling me up since I was sacked . . .

(Pause.)

BALTON: Who?

TERRY *(Looking at Jonathon, sighing. Thinking a moment before replying):* Well, there was the Neams, the Travises, the Lawsons, the Chases . . . about . . . a dozen, really.

(Pause.)

BALTON: I . . . I wonder if . . . if perhaps those—those parents—perhaps they should be on the parents' committee . . .

TERRY *(Doubtful):* Well, if you could get them on . . . yes, I suppose. They might be able to dilute some of Fox's hardliners a bit . . .

MRS. BALTON: Travises, Neams? All of those people? Yes, well, those are all pretty much scholarship names. Everyone knows that. Not quite the same league as the parents thingie, is it?

TERRY *(Smiling):* There we are, Sylvia. You cannot but fail to give yourself away every time.

BALTON: You two, please.

MRS. BALTON: But I think Jonathon is quite right, you really should keep away from it all now. Why don't you think about going back to the farm, love?

BALTON: Mother.

TERRY *(Still smiling, exhausted):* Ah, the farm, yes, it's

always the farm with you, isn't it? Well, that business is all over with now, Sylvia.

MRS. BALTON: Is it really? I remember even as a boy of ten, you were quick with a whip. You had the natives thrashed to a raw and bloody pulp if you didn't get fresh cream in the morning. You loved it all. Horses, guns, all of it. Interesting. Blood always being shed by you, Terry.

TERRY: Times change, Sylvia.

MRS. BALTON: Do they? Still blood being shed by you. Pity.

TERRY: It is what makes you happy, right? Bloodshed?

BALTON: That's enough! God, I'm tired of it all! God, you have no idea how tired of it all, I am, both of you. Damn it, I'm asking for help because I have no idea what I'm doing! I became a schoolteacher because it's quiet and there was no work to be had as a radio actor in Durban. *(Pause)* I just want a bit of peace, damn it, and I'm sure dinner is destroyed.

(He exits.)

MRS. BALTON: Are you eating with us, love? It's just like when you were a boy, you'd come by, causing all sorts of trouble, driving everyone mad. Do you remember the time you were sick into the swimming pool?

TERRY: No.

(She remains seated. Lights down.)

Scene Five

Jonathon's classroom. Hamish Fox, Neville, and Jonathon.

FOX: And why do I see Terry Sinclair's name here? On this agenda?

BALTON: Well, if you let me explain. What it finally—it was more a matter of the senior matriculation tutorials. Not a staff position at all. Just a situation wherein he might come by once a week to coach the seniors. And I've certainly not broached the subject with him, so you needn't worry, Hamish. But the point is, we used to have a ninety-six percent pass rate—the highest. And thanks mostly due to . . . Terry. So, you see, that's why I . . . see?

SUTTER: Yes. Quite. There is that to be considered. Exactly. There is that, isn't there. No, that is true, yes.

FOX: It would not be appropriate, would it, headmaster? *(Pause)* I didn't think it would. Bloody outrageous!

SUTTER: Steady on, Hamish. You've only just this second come from chemotherapy.

BALTON *(Taking out a list):* And I do think perhaps these people should be included on the parents' committee. They've been very good friends to Blenheim.

FOX: *(Taking list and looking at it):* Humph. Well, this lot won't be much good to us, will they. Hum. And perhaps, Jonathon, you might inquire as to Mr. Fidel Castro's availability next?

BALTON: Fidel Cas . . . ah! Hah! Yes. No. No.

FOX: I wonder if perhaps I don't have doubts as to your readiness to be assistant headmaster.

BALTON: Well, I can listen to your doubts, Hamish.

SUTTER: Nobody has any doubts, Jonathon. Hamish, honestly, you mustn't get excited. But Jonathon, what Hamish is trying to say is, I think it's not dissimilar to when we were in the foreign service. One often wanted to accommodate friends. Not unlike any position of choice, eh, Hammy?

FOX: *(After a pause):* In Kenya, they found my sister-in-law tied up to a tree in her garden, with a Mau-Mau's spear inserted through the anus, up the rectum and into the intestines.

SUTTER: Perhaps we might talk about Jonathon's duties.

FOX: Of course, but it's all in the interests of clarity. One becomes concerned that there might be a shift; we might become like one of those cafés where they go on about bizarre ideologies all night. The battles of two hundred years ago have not been concluded, have they? No. Mr. Amin is hanging above our heads, grinning down on us, waiting, waiting! Who's to win? The savage-drum-beating-white-hating-Stalin-worshipping natives, with the Terry Sinclairs of the world urging them on?

SUTTER: Well, of course, exactly the point. First on the agenda is sports practice and seniors. Do they get time off to study or do they buckle down and have sports as well?

FOX: Do you know, when I saw the mad kaffir with the priest's collar up on the podium, I had to smile? There it was, the genesis of decay and rot of our Africa, having spread down the continent like, dare I say it, the cancer in my own spine.

(Pause.)

SUTTER: Indeed. Yes. Very interesting, Hamish. *(Beat)* I say we give 'em time to study and sports be damned. Also, up to you, Jon, to make sure the field's kept trimmed for cricket practice. They're losing balls in the grass, it seems.

FOX: Then there is the small matter of caning, which you have to take over as I can no longer swing my arm.

SUTTER: But mostly just making sure the algae doesn't get too thick in the pool, my boy.

FOX: Also, keeping an eye on the boy's changing room, as the African staff has a tendency to go through the boys' pockets while they're playing sports. Oh, it is a battle, I'm telling you, it is a war . . .

SUTTER: Invitations to parents' day tea, smiles, phone calls about little Evan and Timothy. The usual. Oh, and actually, one job I rather enjoyed; the retaining walls are swarming with lizards and I like to fill up the holes with dry ice and take the pellet gun and get 'em. Nothing like seeing a gecko dashing about in one's sights.

FOX: And Neville and I feel quite strongly that as part of the New Blenheim, it would be very clever to revive yachting club.

BALTON: Yachting club?

FOX: Perfectly fine dinghy in the shed, hasn't seen water in quarter of a century.

BALTON: I see.

FOX: Your responsibility.

BALTON: Me.

SUTTER: Lovely on the bay in December.

FOX: Which won't leave much time for your cinema society, will it?

BALTON: My film society?

FOX: Exactly! Film society. New conditions. Neville and I agree that it's far too—

SUTTER *(Cutting him off):* Yes, well that's quite enough for one day, Hamish. You must be exhausted. We'll continue tomorrow at lunch, perhaps?

BALTON *(Getting up to exit):* I—I have some boys waiting, if I may . . . ?

(He exits rapidly.)

SUTTER: Honestly, Hamish.

FOX: I've just got two things to say.

SUTTER *(Sighing):* Go ahead.

FOX: Not at all like his father. Or mother.

SUTTER: No. A blessing, as I see it. And the other.

FOX: Name the new hall the Christopher and Sylvia Balton Hall, put up a plaque, have a ceremony and proceed forth, eh? You follow me? Considering our current . . . depletion.

SUTTER *(An exhausted whisper):* Yes. That's my point. Isn't it? Exactly.

(Lights down.)

Scene Six

Jonathon's classroom.

BALTON: Well, the fact of it is that, instead of meeting thrice weekly as anticipated, we'll be having these screenings only on Thursday afternoons at half-past three. And you'd best bring with you a sports excuse. Thursday is, of course, junior rugby and third cricket practice and it seems that to be in film society now, you must have a sports excuse. That is the way it goes. And . . . boys on detention are no longer permitted to come to film society in order to work off detention time. *(Pause)* I shouldn't worry too much . . . you can't work off detention time on sports time either, so it's at least somewhat democratic. If you are on detention, you must either remain to work off the detention time at a rate of one point per hour or else you could, as an alternative, erase the detention altogether by being caned twice for each point. The choice is yours. *(Pause)* Mind you, detention boys, if you do decide to get caned instead of detention itself, you would then have time to come to film society. Unless the reason for the punishment is not going to sports practice, in which case, perhaps we'll see you here next term if you have a more agreeable schedule. *(Pause)* Yes, I know. It's all a bit complicated, but what's one to do? *(Pause)* For those of you joining us here for the first time, what happens here is that I show films, no quizzes, no tests . . . occasionally the odd bit of post-film discussion and say . . . if some famous film star happened to be in Durban, well, one of the benefits of the film society is that you might get to meet him. You know, I used to be a radio actor . . . which is quite different from films. *(Pause)* We used to sit in the studio, in fact, the Old Radio Natal studio near the beachfront and one would just lose oneself, really. It was all that one had . . . the rest of the world of no consequence . . . and . . . one might find that coming out . . . coming out into the street from the studio, you might be dazed . . . in the sunlight. It would all seem translucent, shimmering. And my thought was that coming out after film society . . . *(Pause)* might be just a bit like that. *(Pause)* One finds that after Blenheim, the world. *(Pause)* The world. We have a wonderful film about reptiles today.

(Jonathon stands quite still, looking out, and then he slowly moves his hand to the projector and switches it on. Blackout.)

ACT TWO

*Two months later, November. Jonathon, wearing
one of his new suits, angrily slams into the classroom, goes straight to his desk, stops, looks out
for a moment before pulling a bottle of Scotch
from his drawer. He pours a little into a teacup
and waits. Nan rushes in.*

NAN: Jonathon!

BALTON: I don't bloody want to discuss it!

NAN: I only wanted to thank you for putting an end to that
ghastly meeting.

BALTON: I get so angry. I totally humiliated myself.

NAN: No, really, it wasn't that bad. I've always wanted to tell
McNally to go fuck himself.

BALTON: I mean, I'm trying to help them! And they sit there
laughing at me. McNally, this great big, sweaty, huge,
smelly, fat, redfaced baboon sits there snickering at
me? Oh, Christ, and if he doesn't stop going on and on
about his regiment and Angola and his rifle, I'll . . . *(He
stops)* I can't let them upset me.

NAN: You did make rather a dramatic sort of exit. And that
was a hell of a speech you gave.

BALTON: Don't flatter me. You liked it? Totally off the top of
my head, just . . . said what came to mind, really.

NAN: I think it's about time someone said those things,
you're right about it all, pulling together and the
future and cleaning the floors were very true. But you
did go on for half an hour about . . . plasterwork.

BALTON: Did I? I know it's boring, but nobody does anything
about it except me. And I'm doing it all, is the problem! Did you know there are bats—a herd of bats living in the mango trees, attacking boys of the junior
school? The eucalyptus grove has termites the size of
land rovers scurrying about. At any minute we could
have a tree come crashing down, wiping out the entire
first form. Have you seen the swimming pool lately? It
looks like a science experiment—boys go in, have to

send a team to find 'em. We had a monkey come out of the mangrove at cricket practice last week and swipe a ball. The only one we had. And Fox blamed me, I mean—God knows why he's still here, the man's meant to be in bed, but he keeps patrolling like some sort of military zombie—so Fox proceeds to tell me the story of why the British lost the battle of Islan-Dwana because they didn't have hammers or something. I don't know—couldn't open the ammo boxes, nails rusting in the humidity, they all died. I have no idea what it had to do with monkeys swiping cricket balls, but still . . .

NAN *(Trying not to laugh):* It's mad! They're all bloody mad! I'm in charge of fingernail inspection. Yes, they stick out their grubby little digits and wave 'em in front of my eyes.

BALTON *(Beginning to laugh):* Well, that's nothing, because let me tell you first bloody thing this morning, I get a note from Neville. *(A la Sutter)* "Jonathon, in strolling past the junior school toilets, I was assailed by the most unimaginable stench. Please investigate. Best, Nev."

NAN: Well, get out your scuba gear, love. Oh, God, give me a drink, would you?

BALTON *(Pouring her a drink):* So, I go down there, right? It's like the seventh circle of hell. The man is absolutely bloody on target. Water—everywhere. Sort of . . . brown, unfortunately. With little bits of offal floating towards the showers, all of which are sending out huge primeval great mists of . . . steam. I just stood there, hypnotized. The windows have a gruel-like film over them and instead of toilet paper, instead of toilet paper—there are tiny little shreds of . . . newspaper—all over the stalls. Like a hamster's cage. *(Beat)* I swear. The bowel movements of the very young are a total mystery to me.

(Beat.)

NAN: Nobody goes in there to clean? What about Malcom and Montgomery?

BALTON *(Picking up a cane, swinging it, continuing rather*

sadly): Ah, it turns out they've not set foot in there since Fox took ill. Had to fire 'em both. Not the great pleasure it's cracked up to be, but not the horror either.

NAN: Oh, Jonathon, it's all changing, eh?

BALTON: You know something? My dad, horrid as he was, was easily able to delegate authority. I'm going to have to be a bit rough with those pricks in the staff room for a bit.

NAN: Getting into the spirit of the New Blenheim, are we?

BALTON: I just want them to behave well. Be helpful. Less selfish. I never dreamt this job was just one huge campaign. *(Beat)* How does one think, Nan, when thinking has not been necessary?

NAN: If you could tell me—when has it not been necessary, love?

BALTON: They're all watching me. The way I see it, first I get rid of the bats and the termites and the mildew and then we can try and do away with the damn parents' committee and finally, McNally. Let's drink to that, shall we?

NAN: *(After a drink):* You know, I meant to ask you, did I see you shooting at lizards this morning?

BALTON: Oh, no. No, just trying to scare them, really. They . . . you know lizards. Boys see 'em, go mad, can't get 'em back in the classroom. I've had to postpone film society three times in a row. So typical. I said to Nev, at lunch, "The trouble with the world is that nobody has any imagination anymore." And he thought and said, "Yes. A blessing really." *(Pause)* Nobody, that is, except you. Remember we used to go sailing? Wasn't that nice?

NAN: You hated sailing.

BALTON: Did not.

NAN: Please! It was always Ter who did all the work, you were too busy being ill or whining constantly about the waves and capsizing.

BALTON: But *you* enjoyed sailing, didn't you?

NAN: Actually, yes. Jonathon. Why're we talking about sailing?

BALTON: They've been going on for the past two months about wanting me to take on sailing.

NAN: We don't have sailing.

BALTON *(Sighing, not happy):* I'm to help with the Durban Yacht Club Junior Races.

NAN: But what for?

BALTON: Neville seems to think that if a team from Blennies won, we'd attract a new sort. Nautical boys, you know . . .

NAN: I mean . . . *absurd.* Please! That's not the way to get boys!

BALTON: Oh, I don't know about that. Makes sense from a P.R. standpoint. Could be prestigious.

NAN: Typical. But why you, of all people?

BALTON: Neville recalled that the three of us had that dinghy-thingie and I was hoping you might take it on, as I haven't a clue.

NAN: Quite impossible and you know it. I'm teaching all of Terry's classes and half of Fox's. It's hard enough as it is.

BALTON: I understand. But you'd look awfully good to the parents' committee if you took on the damn yachting. They're not very keen on you, still.

NAN: Honestly. Do you think I give a damn about that?

BALTON: It's lovely on the bay in December.

NAN: I've got too much to do as it is and I'm not going to take time away from Terry. And you've stopped calling him . . .

BALTON: That's not fair—he doesn't want to talk to me—you know I've tried.

NAN: Look, I didn't want to tell you, we're having a very bad time. *(Beat)* We've no money left. We were like some sort of package here, two for one. On my wages alone, we're sinking.

BALTON: I had no idea.

NAN: They want us out of the flat. We haven't paid the rent. All our accounts at the shops are shut down. Last week he charged three hundred rand at the bookshop—gave dictionaries out at the school where Bazewo taught. Sat there weeping, passing out books, so really, yachting? Fuck it.

BALTON: Nan, you should've said something to me earlier

because this is the one area where I can help with no problem at all.

(Jonathon takes a checkbook out of his jacket.)

NAN: He went out to see his parents in Zululand, they wouldn't talk to him. What're you doing?

BALTON *(Writing):* I'm giving you a check for five thousand rand.

NAN: No, stop it. I'm not going to take your money. Please, Jonathon, put it away. I don't want a loan.

BALTON: Don't argue with me, it makes no difference to me, I just want you to be happy, I can't sit about and let you—

NAN: *(Cutting him off):* I want a raise.

(Beat.)

BALTON: A raise? Nan, there's no money for plastering, love, let alone raises. Look, just take the check, for Christ's sake. I have this money, my father left it sitting about in boxes!

NAN: No, I can't. You see, we really are leaving. I can't.

BALTON: What do you mean? Leaving? You're not leaving.

NAN: Terry has nothing here. We decided . . .

BALTON: Just take this check and we'll see how you all feel in a few months—

NAN: No! I can't. Look, we're leaving, I'm not going to take five thousand rand from you and bugger off! I want to save something up over six months—and if Blenheim paid me what I deserved, we might be able to.

BALTON: I tried leaving, didn't I? When I went to London, I never told you. I took our stupid, idiotic Lux Radio Theatre tapes. This stupid idea of getting a job in radio drama at the BBC? Insane. Simply insane. And I ended up, you know where? In the bloody isolation ward of some hospital in Chelsea with spinal meningitis. Tapes just lay next to me on the bed.

NAN: Well, if we stay here, Terry'll end up worse off than that!

BALTON: It's ancient, ghastly Paki doctors with shaking hands! That's leaving! It's spinal taps missing the spine, that's leaving! It's a hospital room with wood soap and a clock!

NAN: Oh please, Jonathon, try not to take this as abandoning you—

BALTON: Overseas is vastly overrated! You won't know what to do and you'll be despised, let me tell you, I know it! You'll be all by yourselves! And nobody will help you.

NAN: Well, my husband seems to be asphixiating and nobody here is helping him.

BALTON: Well, just be sure, if you're at some fucking pub in fucking Earl's Court, you tell them when they ask that you're from fucking Sydney. *(Beat)* Damn it, no! I'll be alone, I'll have no one! Please!

NAN: Jonathon, we must—all of us, try and build something as best we can.

BALTON: Right, I shall get you an extra two fifty a week, starting today, all right?

NAN: Jonathon, can you do that? Because you'd be literally saving our lives and—

BALTON: Providing, of course, you were to take on the yachting, starting tomorrow.

NAN: Pardon me? What is this, Jonathon?

BALTON: It's a condition, Nan. A condition. Well, I still have Faber pencils and blotting paper to order. Lots of work still. *(Smiles at a stunned Nan and looks out the window)* There goes the cricket team. Aren't they super. Super.

(He looks at her, as lights fade down.)

Scene Two

Nan and Terry's flat. That night. Terry is sitting, quite still, in his corner chair, as Nan is heard, letting herself in, holding a small bag of groceries and a bag of Chinese food.

TERRY: Well. Good. See me, sitting here? Like an odd and patient breed of dog, oh?

(Nan braces herself, smiles).

NAN: A long and bad, stupid day, Terry. So we'll give it a rest for tonight, right?

TERRY *(Pausing, looking at the bag):* They actually let you take merchandise out of there? I mean, I have to shout for a lamb chop.

NAN: He's not so bad.

TERRY: He is a little Indian racist and I don't think we should be giving him our business.

NAN *(As calm as Terry):* And why now, suddenly?

TERRY *(Shrugging, smiling):* He wouldn't sell me my smokes.

NAN *(Taking a package of cigarettes from the bag):* As long as there's a social context for your boycott . . .

(Pause. She sighs and crosses to him.)

TERRY: There's no such thing as a social context. It's all just chemical, you know. I've been wrong all along. It's all about mommy, daddy, genes and neurons or something.

NAN: I've brought Chinese.

TERRY: Chinese, what a joke. Honorary whites. I wonder, is that all sixty billion of them or just the ones living here. And what on earth would posses a Chinaman to come to South Africa, eh? So. What? Why so late? Watching a flick with old Jonathon? A musical?

(Pause.)

NAN: Ah. I see.

TERRY *(Laughing a bit):* Ah? You see?

NAN: The "ah" of recognition. As in "Ah, he's just spent the day in some sort of rage."

(Pause. Terry nods.)

TERRY *(Looking at the bag of groceries, picks out a tin of tea):* Please, must you buy this cheap kaffir tea? I mean, I don't expect, like, Fortnum's Russian Caravan exactly, but something other than "twin roses." Something that gives one the illusion that there's something mysterious to look forward to.

NAN: What I should do is stop myself rather soon, if I were you, love. Don't you think?

TERRY: The bug is off the phone.

NAN: Really? How—how can you tell?

TERRY: 'Cause they shut the phone off. You never paid them. I actually like this kind of little ironic victory.

NAN: I'll have it on tomorrow.

TERRY: Needn't bother. It's only you or Jonathon—stuttering.

NAN: *What is wrong?*

(Pause.)

TERRY: Jackson was arrested.

NAN: What for?

TERRY: What for? What do you think? You couldn't possibly imagine him out agitating, could you? He was violating the pass laws.

NAN: You . . . you got him out, Ter?

TERRY *(Calmly, but utterly exhausted):* That was interesting. My family name still carries. I think of myself as some sort of pariah, an outcast? But do the Bantu Affairs Police know me? They're busy with their own usual array of murky, oblique affairs. So. I got dressed, very carefully, and I went down to their little corner of hell with its stench of burning rubber reality and I said to the warrant officer, "Listen, mate, that is my bloody servant you've got there and my servant has windows to wash, toilets to clean and a lot to learn, so just hand him over to me and I'll smack him." *(Pause)* And there was this hesitation. The suspicion of my Afrikaaner brethren is boundless. So I stood there and looked him in the eye, rather contemptuously, and addressed him in Afrikaans, "Hey, bloke. My grandfather *ran* your lousy outfit. I deserve a bit of respect and a lot of leeway" . . . and he nods. *(Pause)* This man has never heard of Blenheim. *(Pause)* And he hands me Jackson.

NAN: So—he's alright?

TERRY: Oh, fine.

NAN: Jesus, it's endless.

TERRY: Isn't it? Of course, you've just come from a "long, bad, and stupid day" yourself.

NAN: Actually, I have come from a pretty shoddy bit of manipulation and humiliation and it has left me feeling pretty stupid, so Christ knows, I don't need to walk in here and be insulted by you.

TERRY *(Picking up letter from the table beside the chair):* Please don't tell me about your lousy day at Blenheim and your humiliations. Please. Not now. *(Pause)* Because I have just received a letter from Victor Frame offering a job at the Esquella Americana in Rio de Janeiro and I can't take it because we don't have enough money to get out!

NAN: Victor Frame? Let me see . . .

TERRY: Blenheim. Class of '61. Was on the cricket team when I was captain. Worshipped me.

NAN: Well, let's start again. Look. I've got a raise so if we put some money away, we could go in about six months . . .

(Pause.)

TERRY: Oh please, you must be joking. What pack of lies did they feed you? A raise? It's impossible. They're on the verge of shutting down by now and I did it to them.

NAN: Wait a second. I'm telling you, Jonathon's got me a raise. Look, we can get out, it's all you talk about, come on.

TERRY: Jonathon . . . got you . . . a raise. Something's wrong here, Nan. It doesn't make sense. Come on, you're smart, what do you mean? Have you seen the place? It looks like a Moorish ruin. Jonathon? Raise? What? He could show you a double feature, but a raise . . . it's a lie, it's one of those things they say . . . *(Beat)* I mean, don't be naïve.

NAN: No, no, no. You don't understand. It was a very specific transaction, Terry. He made me take on yachting in return for the raise.

TERRY: Yachting, oh, now we're into sheer fantasy. Yachting, my dear, you couldn't put up a spinnaker if there was one sticking out your bum. Don't be absurd. These boys'd kill you out there! You want to end up floating face down in Durban harbor, with half the school dancing on the prow? It's a con job! Yachting.

NAN: Hey. You sit about here all day, doing God knows what. I mean, I have no idea. You say you can't read anymore, you can't think, so what? I'm telling you, Terry, I'm tired to death of it now, it makes up for what we've been losing. All you talk about is leaving, now we can do it. Write back to Victor Frame and ask him to give you some time. I don't know. Brazil sounds lovely, anything, Terry.

TERRY: Two-fifty? Well, seeing as you got a raise, why don't you get Jackson back?

(Beat.)

NAN: What do you mean?

TERRY: Do you know, I spent our last cent getting him sprung? Yes. I let him go, Nan. I sent the man packing.

NAN: I don't understand. Are you trying to tell me you've fired Jackson?

TERRY: Yes, I fired Jackson. Yes!

NAN: Jesus, what the hell is the matter with you? Where the hell do you think the man's going to go? Do you know how long he'll last out there? He has nothing! He has nowhere!

TERRY *(Viciously, snaps back):* Yes, and we have no money! And Christ, it's enough of this crap, people padding about furtively, making little plans, this miasma, and I'm so sick of it, I don't care anymore! Waiting for the dusty green kaffir bus—you should've seen him—I stood here, watching him from this window. Bus after bus, he stood there, couldn't move! Weeping! I mean, finally, I couldn't watch any more. Goodbye Jackson, this stick figure, frozen, terrified. I hate it.

NAN: Oh, Terry, how far do you want to fall? How much . . . pain do you think you can inflict? I don't think I can take much more.

TERRY: Even with your raise, we're trapped. How much can we save? We owe money all over town! It'll take a year to pay all the bills and I'm not going to run out on every little shopkeeper in this town. If that's what you expect. Save? We're in the black hole of Calcutta.

NAN: No. I understand. *(She sits down)* I've really been so stupid, it's so clear to me now. Here I've been thinking, it'll be okay once we leave. But the fact of it is, you really don't want to go anywhere, do you? Except a little walk along the beachfront now and then.

TERRY: Pardon?

NAN: Oh, don't. "Pardon?" Please. I mean, it's all very easy. Jackson's not the frozen and terrified one, really.

TERRY: Let me tell you, I'm being practical, you come in talking about a raise like it's the answer to all our problems, big deal. And that schoolmistress tone may work with your home-fucking-economics class, but don't ever bring it in here.

NAN: No. Talk to me, don't—

TERRY *(Shouting, cutting her off)*: Then don't you play at Freud! Don't play at amateur ladies charity tea-shrink-contest-runner up! God, none of your pat little answers and—and the kind of sympathy you reserve for a—

NAN: —how dare you? I mean, all you do is take these positions, I mean, talk about clothing yourself in stances, please. At first it's funny, this man rushing out to buy the Beatles, fine, funny, rush out to smoke dope, hipper, always, than all of us. *(Beat)* But the thing is, you really love it all. Blenheim, this beachfront, this small world here. It's just this fading of honesty, Terry. I'm sorry. Just stop lying to me! I don't care about you changing your mind, Christ knows I don't want to pack up and move to bloody Brazil. It's the posing. Do you understand? You don't have to do that, we've been married long enough. Just say, "I want to stay." Because I want you to understand, this whole . . . wretched . . . business has been breaking my heart.

(Long pause.)

TERRY: Not much else to say, eh? It's . . . you know, the times I—I go for a walk, pass Blenheim and I'll just stop, remembering what it was like to be a boy there. Holding my cricket kit. In the same spot, fifteen years ago. So happy, so amazed a boyhood could be so perfect. I just stand there, here I am, in my thirties, and reduced to memory already. *(Beat)* Well, tell me what I should do then? I mean, I don't . . . I don't know where I belong, is the thing, I thought as a kid, "I'm a gentleman farmer, fine." And then, "Oh, I'm an academic" and I detest the academics—so fine, radical. I'm a radical, right, great. Make a little radical gesture, hope to join that club and someone's dead, so—I don't know what to do . . . I would go back. I would go back and teach. I mean, finally, I only belong at Blenheim, just like Jonathon. I let it . . . destroy me. Is it so bad? To want to go back? Is it such a . . . defeat?

NAN: No, of course not. No. It hasn't destroyed you.

(She holds him.)

TERRY *(Closing his eyes, shaking his head)*: I would've . . . liked to have shown you the Amazon, because you know, it's going. It's the mining. *(Beat)* It's . . . *(Lights fade down. He gasps, reaches for her)* a whole other world . . .

Scene Three

Mrs. Balton's flat. Sutter and Mrs. Balton. Late afternoon.

MRS. BALTON: You see, if you look out over the verandah— that little red thingie in the water?

SUTTER: I can't possibly see that far anymore, Sylvia.

MRS. BALTON: Shark-net buoy. Swim past there and they'll eat you up like they did that girl a few months ago.

SUTTER: Never cared for the water myself.

MRS. BALTON: Christopher and I used to swim out for miles.

SUTTER: Extraordinary.

MRS. BALTON: How's the farm?

SUTTER: Haven't been for ages. Joyce has shingles again.

MRS. BALTON: You did the right thing, holding on to it.

SUTTER: It's just the house and some acres—had to sell some more this term, in fact.

MRS. BALTON: City is becoming harder to bear, daily. Like Bombay and Cairo.

SUTTER: I knew we'd end up on the farm one day. Still have the same herd boy. Ninety-one. Isn't doing much now—lives in the same shack. Bring him his tea and biscuit myself when I'm there. Sheds a tear every time. You'll come for Christmas, as usual, of course.

MRS. BALTON: Very upsetting seeing my old farm just across from yours. In the country, one can still smell old Africa. Clean, English sort of Africa, hint of something else out of range. India

SUTTER: Well, that's all gone now. Here in the city as well.

MRS. BALTON: But one doesn't want to end one's days in the city. Remember what this town used to be like? Banquets at the Oyster Box Hotel?

SUTTER: The old beachfront. Three Monkeys coffeehouse? Remember?

MRS. BALTON: The old Durban, the old style. Indian waiters with sashes about their waists and bright red thingies on their heads.

SUTTER: Jonathon is doing a remarkable job, Sylvia.

MRS. BALTON: And you're surprised?

SUTTER: A bit, yes. So soon.

MRS. BALTON: It shouldn't surprise you; he's Christopher's and my son.

SUTTER: True, but at Blenheim one sees many sons. Even Hamish Fox is happy.

MRS. BALTON: Hamish Fox's happiness could not be of less consequence.

SUTTER: Yes, well it is to me. My heavy, eh? Syl, love. We need that rather large push we've all been talking about right now and, of course, we're asking certain families to help.

MRS. BALTON: Nev. Love. The point is this—Blenheim needs more than a mere push. You are on the verge of bankruptcy, are you not?

SUTTER: Exactly where we are, yes.

MRS. BALTON: You've continued to lose old boy support, have you not?

SUTTER: That's true, yes.

MRS. BALTON: And the new families have formed some sort of parents' committee, have they not?

SUTTER: Sylvia, must we negotiate like Jews? Tell me your terms. I'll tell you if they can be met.

MRS. BALTON: I am prepared to make a permanent endowment.

SUTTER: Please go on.

MRS. BALTON: You must retire within twelve months and Jonathon must be made headmaster.

SUTTER: I thought it might be something like that, dear.

MRS. BALTON: Or I could take my money and go off and buy some little farm somewhere, which would leave very little for endowments. I'll need to ask the accountant, Mr. Schorr.

SUTTER: Jonathon as headmaster. May I remind you, when I bought Blenheim, your husband lent me the money?

MRS. BALTON: A lot. With no qualms and no interest.

SUTTER: Exactly. And I thought I could build a gentleman's sort of place with a rigorous approach to education and yet, at the same time, be rather humane. Wasn't that the oddest youthful presumption?

MRS. BALTON: I used to find sugarcane farming romantic. One learns perspective, Neville. Jonathon is the only way.

SUTTER: And when I purchased Blenheim from McFarquire, it really was rather nightmarish. 1936. So primitive, floggings day and night, forced marches into the bush barefoot, smell of rotten wood rising up to one's nostrils at every turn. Boys with infections and bleeding welts from beatings and fully one-third of them with broken limbs from rugby against the Afrikaaner school. Which they never lost. And the staff, Sylvia? You and Christopher never really knew them, you never mingled with the hoi polloi, did you?

MRS. BALTON: I'm sure they were most remarkable men, Neville.

SUTTER: The original Blenheim staff? They came with the

place when I bought it. Religious hysterics exiled from England by their families—fat rejects with quivering, bluish lips, breathing heavily after the little boys, shell-shocked Great War fodder, reliving the trenches in the classroom . . . the flotsam and jetsam of the empire, but you know—the truly mind-boggling thing is that Blenheim has never been as popular as it was then! And I gradually replaced that clutch of barnyard animals with a more reasonable lot. And felt so proud when Jonathon and Terry came on. It seemed the final dissolution of the old Blenheim. And look where it's got me.

MRS. BALTON: I shouldn't punish myself quite so hard, Nev. Could always pack it in, close the doors. Turn it into a nursing home. I'm told those do rather well.

SUTTER: Ah, yes. There you are. Built something, got to defend it. Jonathon'll be head, of course, Sylvia. But don't ask me for a date; he's not ready yet.

MRS. BALTON: I do think next year is sufficient, actually. And I should like, if I may, to have something in writing.

(Pause.)

SUTTER: I beg your pardon?

MRS. BALTON: A simple contract, Neville. It's business, Neville. Business.

(Pause.)

SUTTER: Look at who we are. And look, Sylvia, at what we are and tell me when a handshake has not been utterly sufficient.

(Beat.)

MRS. BALTON: But, Neville, it is precisely because of who we are and what we are that I *do* want a contract.

(Pause.)

SUTTER: I see.

(Sylvia offers him her pen, as the lights fade down.)

Scene Four

NAN *(Addressing her class):* When I asked for essays on the Zulus, I wasn't looking for detailed accounts of native laziness in your father's factory, Cleasby. Nor am I interested in your examination of native killing techniques. It's tired and I'm tired of it. It's as if your Africa were some kind of Atlantis, with drums and spears. It's not the one we're in. *(Pause)* I thought we might then, try these essays again? Somehow demythologized, okay? I was thinking—as I was reading them—I was thinking back, remembering, because my family had a number of maids as I was growing up. And there was a blur, a period of faces, names—I can't connect, but there was Edna. And she had been with us for some years—this good-natured, virtually invisible friend. Whose life was actually far more complicated than ours. My father did nothing, really. There was a vastness of leisure time, a morass. *(Pause)* And Edna had this husband who worked in the mines whom she saw with less and less frequency over the years. My mother found his presence—his dusty, coarse skin—upsetting, even if he was only to spend the night in the little room in the back. He was never actually forbidden; it was a kind of subtle discouragement. And—it was the same with her children—who had been cast out to the grandmother's little squash patch and mud hut in Zululand . . . somewhere where everyone might be reunited at Christmas for a couple of days or so. Eventually, the circumstances of this thwarted, enslaved life, all the wretchedness, made functioning as a human being harder and harder. *(Pause)* And of course, as it becomes harder to function as a human being, it makes being a good servant pretty much an impossibility. *(Pause)* She became moody. Forgetting to bathe, becoming, finally, something of a darkness in our home. And as Edna's personality became that of a toast-burning hag, I started to develop an intense dislike for her. There was a point where my family's main source of bored, wintry amusement—the height of morbidity, finally, was to, over dinner, discuss the decline of Edna, discuss it, in fact, as she served. *(Pause)* And, of course, she began to sour. Her human-ness became overwhelming, like meat left out far too long. And when the dimension of her life overtook our own, she was finally, simply sent away. *(Pause)* And the next week, it began again with a new servant. So really, I mean, this kind of Atlantis you describe, it hardly does credit to the real one which has its own violence, its own terrors, quite independent of Fox's Africa of guns and war. That Africa—denies what we are. Our own brand of callousness. Surely there have been lives that have meant something to you? And I would very much like to know about that. Do you understand this?

(Hamish Fox has entered moments before and stands in the doorway.)

FOX: Ergh.

NAN: Oh! Hello . . . ? Class, please stand up.

FOX: Sit. I just came to fetch some items, if you don't mind, Mrs. Sinclair. I'd like to have my goodbyes with the boys, please.

NAN *(Starting to exit)*: Yes, of course. Please. Go ahead.

FOX: Many years of rubbish collected in here. You'll be amazed, Mrs. Sinclair, when you come and fetch it all.

NAN: Yes. I expect I will.

(She exits.)

FOX *(To class)*: When writing an essay, every thought must be crystal clear. Picture the sentence before you. Does it look correct? The comma in the right place? Spelling accurate? And the thought itself. How is that? Your penmanship must not waver because when it does, it weakens the idea. And, of equal importance, is that you do not let an inkblot foul the paper. Nothing is so dam-aging as an inkblot, like some vile black stain, occlud-ing the light, breaking clarity. Make certain that the ink is running smoothly through the body of the pen to the nib which must never be bent. The nib must be as clean as the surgeon's scalpel—as vital an instrument. Imprint of the manufacturer must always be visible on the nib or blots will occur. Do not put red ink into a pen which has had blue or black. Rather, keep three pens. If you cannot afford three pens, then you must wash the one thoroughly before putting in the new color of ink. From the blue book, learn three new words a day. You must be able to convey the clarity of your intent under fire, in the office, on the field; clarity of expression equals success. Your privilege is this education which separates you from the savage and, in the years ahead, this will be a most formidable weapon. *(Pause)* I would also say, if I may be a bit more personal for a moment, that I would prefer it if nobody visited me in hospital—a strain on all parties that is best avoided. So, without further rigmarole, I shall see you, I'm certain, after Boxing Day when I shall tell you about the idiocy of the Maginot Line. And Douglas Bader, the war hero with no legs.

(Fox exits slowly, as lights fade down.)

Scene Five

Jonathon's classroom. Jonathon and Sutter.

SUTTER: You must understand, this is very upsetting.

BALTON: Oh dear.

SUTTER: What the hell's the matter with her?

BALTON: Well now, we don't know exactly what went on, do we?

SUTTER: Hamish Fox—Hamish Fox comes in and tells me of some sort of madwoman speech in social bloody history class?

BALTON: Yes. This from a man who's less evolved than the creature for which he's named.

SUTTER: Don't be clever, Jonathon. The Mowatts. The Ashburnhams and the Halliwells have all decided to withdraw their boys at end of term if nothing is done.

BALTON: Look, if Blenheim is to move forward, don't you think we should be permitted to do so without the constant terrorization of our staff by hysterics? Don't you agree, Nev?

SUTTER: Of course I fucking agree! But the point is, that Mowatt woman is the most fertile female in Natal. I was looking forward to another four boys at least! I mean, the whole business has gone way, way too far!

BALTON: Sometimes boys come back, don't they?

SUTTER *(Scornful):* Oh, thank you. *(He stumbles over a chair)* Christ—I can't see! She must've known that with things the way they are, this would cost her her damn job!

BALTON: I was expecting something like that—are you serious?

SUTTER: Deadly serious. I'm too tired of it. Why the hell should we be destroyed over this? We've all seen fine boys come out of here—I'm not going to just sit here and watch the whole place eroding. The parents' committee may be repulsive, but they're absolutely correct; we need a purge—a bloodletting—their words exactly!

BALTON: Well, then I have the right idea—fire McNally, hell, I'll do it! Let's be bloody aggressive about it—bring back Terry! And if—if you stand there, telling me that he's a fucking communist, I'll be out the door myself, old man, I swear it!

(Pause. Sutter raises his eyebrows, regards Jonathon.)

SUTTER: I know he's not a communist. But that's not the point. He could be a cross between Aristotle and Jesus Christ for all I care. He's not coming back. I've got to have surgery on my eyes or I shall end up being led about by a water spaniel. I'm going to Cape Town for surgery and I'm leaving you in charge and I have decided, Jonathon, that it is to be your responsibility to end this business. She's to have her last day on Friday. And be gone after lunch.

BALTON: It is just giving in to those dull horrors who drop their kids off here every morning! Why? Why, Neville?

SUTTER: It is not for further discussion. I'm exhausted. It has been decided.

BALTON: But why must I do it, then?

SUTTER *(Icy):* Because I, Jonathon, am going blind.

BALTON: But I can't even—I can't do it—

SUTTER *(Thundering):* No discussion! I am dead from discussion! And diplomacy! It . . . is . . . over. And I want new septic tanks, please, Jonathon, by the time I return. The smell of offal around here is overwhelming. Joyce can't entertain the parents' committee.

BALTON *(After a pause):* I ask you this. One question, Neville. What is left?

(Pause.)

SUTTER: What is left, Jonathon, is Blenheim.

(Lights fade down.)

Scene Six

Early evening. The bench by the wall. Terry is sitting alone. He is clean-shaven, calm and well-dressed in khaki twills, a striped shirt and sweater.

BALTON *(Offstage):* Terry.

TERRY: It's very lovely, isn't it, when it's this quiet?

BALTON *(Entering, his jacket carried over his shoulder, a cigar in his teeth):* My favorite times, early morning and in the evening after the little buggers have left. When it's empty. Good to see you, Ter.

TERRY: Yes. You look well. This is all agreeing with you, eh?

(Pause.)

BALTON *(Quietly):* Yes it is. I showed myself a film just now. Mr. Blandings builds his . . . dream house. Very sad, funny. Sort of. Hmn.

TERRY *(Leaning over, picks up a stone):* You know, once when I was a boy, I found a spearhead here.

BALTON: I remember. But I think, in fact, it was planted by Fox. *(Pause)* Are you well? You look better.

TERRY *(Shrugging, embarrassed):* I think. Yes. Been a hell of a time . . . I . . . *(Pause)* They're building Balton Hall?

BALTON: A brilliant and aggressive move on Neville's part. Sort of a cross between Versailles and Walter Gropius. Daring. He's gone off. Left me in charge. They're doing something to his corneas.

TERRY: Yes. And left you to do as you will?

BALTON: . . . I suppose . . . yes. He has.

TERRY: Jon—I had an interview, ah, at the University of Natal. But the poor old head of English and Speech and Drama, just a tired, fucked old bloke—they've got half his faculty gone—whispered in my ear, "Love to take you on, Ter. But it's just not on, old boy. *(Pause)* Can't . . . take any chances now," he said.

BALTON: Ah.

TERRY: Yes. They have their own troubles. A Jesuit in the law school arrested.

BALTON: Yes. I read it. Look up there, up the hill—they're burning sugarcane . . . smell it?

TERRY *(Looking off left):* I know—I was thinking before you came, watching it. It's like the huge, roaring wall of flame between us and the rest of the world. How do you ever get through it? The fiery wall of mythology? McNally's stories of Negroes descending en masse from Harlem, Fox's Pakis and Arabs taking over London . . . look at that fire. It's growing and growing. The hatred for the rest of the world. And how do you find passage through it?

BALTON: I wonder. You were trying, weren't you? Somehow. To connect . . . at the centenary? It's one of the things I love in the cinema—the movies. *(Pause)* That thing, heroism in unexpected places. Look. Give this to Nan, will you? I missed her this afternoon, meeting Sutter. Her raise—first check.

(Jonathon reaches into his pocket and hands Terry a check.)

TERRY: They've got you signing checks now, eh?

BALTON: Yes. A heady feeling indeed.

TERRY: Not much more to give you then, is there?

BALTON: It all seems to be working out, somehow, for once, I think.

TERRY *(Embarrassed)*: I have, uhm . . . *(He stands up)* God. I should just say this. I'd like to come back. I grew up here, I don't really know where else to go. I know you've got some leeway now. *(He looks away. Thinks)* I miss you. I miss the place. I miss being liked by certain boys. The ones who . . . can make you laugh. The ones who're worth it. I miss 'em. I'm standing here now, it's the only place I feel comfortable. *(Beat)* It'll be very quiet. I don't like doing this to you, but I've always helped you, Jonathon, I've never really, not that I can remember, asked you for very much. You know, when you moved here from the farm, you asked if I would come too. So now, I'm asking you, bring me back. This is the only place I know how to fight that fire.

(Long pause.)

BALTON *(Quietly):* Yes, good. You can start in the new year.

(Lights fade down.)

Scene Seven

A cemetery by the Indian Ocean. It stretches off—a pastoral green under an intense sun. In the distance, there is the crashing sound of waves hitting rocks. Jonathon and Sutter enter, the latter with a patch over one eye.

BALTON: Neville. Do you think you should rest? You've only just got off an airplane.

SUTTER: No. I shall rest tomorrow at the farm. *(He pulls his flask out of his blazer)* Drink?

BALTON: No. Thank you.

SUTTER: Huge cemetery, isn't it?

BALTON: Never been in here.

SUTTER *(Pointing off):* The old Durban faces—all out. Seems the only time we see one another is when one of us dies. Was a time when, instead of a grave, we met at the cricket finals. I do wish more of the old boys had shown. To say goodbye to Hamish. This saddens.

BALTON: You didn't see them! The Mowatts, the Cleasbys.

SUTTER: Must be my eyes.

BALTON: How was the airplane?

SUTTER: Joyce was bilious and broke out in shingles. A spell of bad luck, eh? Her shingles. My eyes, spending money madly . . .

BALTON: But it should turn about in the spring.

SUTTER: Wish I had a biscuit with my whisky. This eye treatment? They use a laser, burns a hole, you can hear the eye sizzling like bacon. They insist it's painless, but really, it's hell.

BALTON: But useful, eh?

SUTTER: You did a remarkable job, making Hamish's funeral arrangements and all.

BALTON: Yes. And I've put a nice Christmas tree in Assembly Hall.

SUTTER: You know, I looked at my body in the mirror before the funeral. I'm all white, all soft. Little veins, like a tea doily under the white. Like a map. An old and tattered map. Up my left leg is a vein that looks remarkably like the Blue Nile. Been up 'em both.

BALTON: Ah.

SUTTER: Quite interesting, seeing the old crowd here, out to bury Hamish. Because I looked at them and they're white and veiny too. Cumberland told me that he had little capillaries exploding all over his left side. Showed me. Looked like Ghana, from years and years, his doctor told him, of drinking cane spirits. Gotta stop drinking, they tell him, and we had a bit of a laugh over that. I mean—what's the point, at this stage, eh? *(Pause)* What a pathetic bunch of old men and their stray wives, standing about in a cemetery. A clutch of rheumy-eyed, sodden, yellow-toothed old gentlemen farmers and their distorted wives, all of us with nowhere to go. And yet, look out there—the sulphuric, red-streaked, mad sea. Pounding on the rocks. A dead end for me. *(Pause)* Not only have you not fired her, but you've given her a raise. I looked at the ledger before I came. Why?

BALTON *(Sighing):* I'm sorry. Well then, here we are. Should I pack my things?

SUTTER: Let's discuss it.

BALTON: Oh, let's not, Nev. Let's not be clever, shall we? Just fire me, if you're going to.

SUTTER: Jonathon. You needn't stand there like a fifth former about to get a hiding.

BALTON: But, Neville, you see, I've always been terrified of those who judge—always wanted to please authority. First father, then mother, Terry . . . and now you.

SUTTER: I know.

(Pause. Jonathon takes a deep breath.)

BALTON: Neville. Do you honestly believe that I do not know why I was made assistant head? All it took was the tiny bit of intuition I've got. Mother. It's shameful, Nev, to think I'd be so dull-witted as to not understand. And so, at the point of realization—the epiphany—one feels pretty dreadful, pretty damn ugly. Incapable, swindled. And for you to assume utter unquestioning on my part, the absolute certainty of my taking orders, makes me feel utterly pathetic.

SUTTER: Not my intent, Jonathon.

BALTON: So why not help my only friends? Two people who have had the best intentions—the most fair-minded . . . you know why I am friends with Terry? Because since we were boys—he could always be good enough for the both of us. And Nan—they're not like us. Why not help two such friends?

(Pause.)

SUTTER: And what about politics, Jonathon?

BALTON: Politics?

SUTTER: Exactly.

BALTON: And after all this time, why is it . . . that *now* . . . I should suddenly find myself involved . . . in of all things, *your* . . . politics?

SUTTER: An education, isn't it?

BALTON: Because, if we're all to end up white, corroded bodies at the edge of the sea, I'd rather not have the memory of my own cowardice, my own shrivelling-up. Anything, anything other than this exhaustion, this—depletion—this ceaseless, repulsive dignity.

SUTTER: I agree completely.

BALTON: But isn't firing Nan absolutely cowardly? This is what I've always despised about you. About all of you. Words mean nothing.

SUTTER: No. Not nothing. Just less than they should. Jonathon, lad. Listen, please.

BALTON: But you see, I think—I think . . . it's gone far enough. Let's stop, shall we? I've had quite enough.

SUTTER: No cinematic histrionics, please.

BALTON: Neville, you don't understand.

SUTTER: It is you again, who does not understand. Though it is refreshing to hear you make so much sense for once. Look. Your mother does help us. True. But your mother's money did not make you assistant headmaster.

BALTON: Oh, yes it did.

SUTTER: No. Though it is convenient for her to think that she protects you. It is you that I have thought of. Your well-being and Blenheim's. I have built and defended that place and it's virtually killed me. It's more, ultimately, than just the dry bones of mere ritual. I could've found another way, if I thought you were wrong. You're far more interesting than either of your parents. Your mother is a viper. And your father was like a killer whale, gulping in air. So do me this favor. This thing. Fire Nan and then you're headmaster of Blenheim.

BALTON: I won't do it to Nan.

SUTTER: It is your only chance, your only hope. There are, you must realize, very definite, very cogent reasons for this business. Do you remember what I told you when you took assistant head? "You find yourself becoming more the representative. And you've got to acknowledge what it is you're representing." I need to know now, what and who it is you are representing. You must let Nan go—then I'll know you're ready.

MRS. BALTON *(Entering):* That's very good, Neville. I think you're right.

BALTON: Oh, Mother. I'm not interested in discussing it with you. Look. Let me put it clearly. Just fire me.

MRS. BALTON: It's the coldest of worlds out there. I've told you many times. But you've not listened. If you left Blenheim, how would you spend your days? *(Pause)* You know, don't you? You'd end up serving me tea on a tray, just like nanny, wasting away in her room. You think you are lonely now, but without Blenheim, the days will just stretch ahead of you agonizingly, Jonathon. And you will find yourself an old man with frail hands, outrageous scarves, in an oceanfront flat, eating pudding on a white plate. Absolutely—irredeemably isolated.

BALTON: That's not true!

MRS. BALTON: As if in a hole. And your pleasure? You will go to the cinema alone, purchase your ticket, sit in the dark and you'll walk out a little closer to death.

BALTON: No.

MRS. BALTON: No. You can't do that anymore, can you, Jonathon? You have begun to enjoy this new experience. This power. Have you not? Your new suits? You are more careful in your bathing, in combing your hair. You have been admired, effective. And it would end.

BALTON: Listen to yourself, Mother.

MRS. BALTON: I cannot allow this to happen. Because I won't be here to protect you. Be realistic.

BALTON: Like you? It doesn't interest me.

MRS. BALTON: You are destined to be lonely, Jonathon. It is only a matter of degree. The choice is yours. Life is such a trifle, such a small thing. And one is left with what little one has built.

BALTON: What have we built, Mother?

MRS. BALTON: A relatively quiet, somewhat safe, permanently endowed home for my boy. Blenheim School for Boys.

BALTON: A home? With no friends. Like our home, Mother.

MRS. BALTON: Do you know what would happen if Nan

stayed on and you brought back Terry? Could you build the Blenheim you want? Nobody else wants it. And you didn't even have the stamina to sustain your film society. You would destroy yourself for two people who will live without you and whom you can never have.

(Long pause.)

BALTON: You are a brutal and savage woman, which you know. But what nobody has ever told you is that, actually, you are an extraordinarily shallow one as well.

(Jonathon turns to exit.)

SUTTER: Jonathon!

(Jonathon stops.)

Whatever you decide now—you are going to have to live with it. Forever. There is no going back. Do you understand?

(Jonathon walks off. Pointing off.)

Look over the wall, Sylvia. The Hindu are burning their dead. Let's go and have a look, shall we?

(Lights fade down.)

Scene Eight

Jonathon's classroom. A small Christmas tree stands in one corner. Jonathon is at his desk. On the blackboard is a note: "Classes dismissed in order to attend the funeral of Mr. Fox." Terry and Nan enter.

TERRY: Jonathon.
BALTON: Ah, there you are. Nice funeral, wasn't it?
NAN: No. There was hardly anyone there for him. I mean— not to sentimentalize him, but . . .
TERRY: He had nobody, really. I could use a drink.

BALTON: Frightening, isn't it? And sad. Did you know that he shrunk to the size of a pygmy before he finally died?

NAN: Are you alright? You look pale.

BALTON: This was only my second funeral. My father's the only other. You were very fond of my father, weren't you, Terry? Horses and all that. But you didn't really know him. Did you?

TERRY: . . . No. I mean, the public version only. Right? You look like you could use a drink, Jonathon . . .

BALTON: No. Just tired out. I was thinking of the farm. Every Saturday night, Father'd give one of the cows to the natives. A treat. Few farms did that. But actually, it was no sacrifice, just a small feeble animal. And yet, cane-cutters, herd boys, all of them . . . would look forward to Saturday night. The compound would come alive. That mad Zulu pop music on the Bantu radio. I'd sit in nanny's lap, watching. It was all very festive. *(Beat)* I was mostly interested in the killing of the cow. Used to be, they used a knife and that was vivid, very much a thing of the bush. To see the creature's dull eyes flashing, hooves scraping at the dirt as the knife was led across the throat—and the blood running into a gourd on the ground. But the part that fascinated me the most was when it was dead. Its evisceration. The skin drawn slowly back and the veins exposed, black blood clotting into the reddish dust of the compound which would be dead quiet, somber. Little ivory-colored and purple-hued sacks filled with bile and acid and urine. Balloons of undigested grass, bones cracked and muscles pulsing gently as a fire was readied, and the tongue, the great curled muscle, unravelled, cut out, and the teeth and jaw laid bare. *(Pause)* But it is one Saturday in particular that I remember. It was my birthday and I was given the honor of killing the cow. I was eleven. The knife was dispensed with and my father gave me a pistol with tiny silver-tipped bullets. I was to blow out the brains from a little spot between the eyes and this death had none of the ritual of the knife. It was an assassination and I believe the natives knew this. Unbearable to have this cow led to me, docile and uncomplaining. She was tied to a post with a little strand of rope and I tried to do the thing very quickly. But you see, I did not do a proper job of it. And the bullet ricocheted off her skull and down into the jaw—this shattered pulp of bone and blood through which she screamed, you see, as I recall it. And tore loose from her feebly tied rope. And there she was with saliva and plasma all about, bolting into the cane fields, everyone stunned. She was gone. And I stood there. Frozen. *(Pause)* And I looked up and saw my father standing on the verandah of the main house with my mother—and he whispered something to her and went inside and nanny came to me. And of course, by this time, I was crying. The natives staring at their feet—mortified. No laughter—which might have been preferable. *(Pause)* And then my father came out of the house with his shotgun, got on his horse and rode into the field, and there was a single muffled blast and nanny put me to bed. A quiet supper that night, no singing or dancing, and of course, not long after, we moved into the city—my mother's idea. So I was just thinking about my father and all.

(Pause.)

TERRY: Funerals. It's death . . . that makes us think. Not life, usually, unfortunately. It's natural.

BALTON: Natural. No, it has nothing to do with nature, Terry. And also, after all is said and done, after all our reasoning and . . . grasping, searching . . . nobody really . . . cares.

TERRY: Well, I used to think that.

BALTON: No. You don't understand, Terry. You can't come back.

TERRY: What's happened?

BALTON: I've been made headmaster. And Nan, you are . . . fired.

NAN: Are you telling me—I don't understand. You just fired me?

TERRY: That's right. I understand. They've made you head-master.

BALTON: No you don't understand. At all. You've always said, "There's something terribly odd about Jonathon. He's baffled by it all" . . . but you are wrong. I am not at all baffled by it all.

NAN: No. There's nothing you can say.

BALTON: Nan, remember when I asked you, "Must you leave?" You said . . . "We must all of us . . . try and build something as best we can"? That is what I have done.

NAN: Yes, you have. Well, you will be alone, Jonathon.

BALTON: You see? I cannot live with that anymore! These judgments. The echo of some whispered judgment on a verandah. All your talk, I have to say no to it. Your demands, your politics—the rightness of your politics, I say no, and I will survive. You have this idea. It is of change and the future and hope and prevailing. And you hand me a gun. *(Beat)* It's so easy for you to judge me. You hand me a gun, point it at my head. And watch. *(Beat)* No. Say whatever you like. *(Almost smiles, almost self-mocking)* Say I am a monster. In this room, the projector gone, the true product of Blenheim. Blenheim's monster. Skipping, lurching down the halls, really. As a boy. And as a man. Say anything.

TERRY *(After a moment, shaking his head):* Happy . . . New Year, Jonathon.

(They look at him for a moment. He looks back. They exit.)

BALTON *(A whisper):* Yes. It is.

(Jonathon walks over to the desk. Picks up a box of Christmas tree decorations and goes to the tree. He places a small star on the pinnacle. And then, from the box, he takes a tin of artificial snow. Which he begins to spray all over the tree and, after a moment, slowly, straight up into the air, over his head. And he lifts his hands to catch the white powder as it filters down upon him, swirling to the floor, a small storm.)

The
Substance of
Fire

To my parents

Playwrights Horizons, Inc., New York City, produced *The Substance of Fire* Off Broadway in 1991.

World premiere presented at the Long Wharf Theatre, Arvin Brown, Artistic Director, M. Edgar Rosenblum, Executive Director, 1990.

Workshopped at Naked Angels.

Characters

MARTIN GELDHART
SARAH GELDHART
ISAAC GELDHART
AARON GELDHART
MARGE HACKETT

Time and Place

Act One

A conference room, Kreeger/Geldhart Publishers, Manhattan, Spring, 1987

Act Two

An old apartment in Gramercy Park, three and a half years later

The Substance of Fire

ACT ONE

Spring, 1987.

A conference room, Kreeger/Geldhart Publishers, Manhattan, in the Broadway-23rd Street area. There is a conference table, five chairs, some filing cabinets. There are many books. Sarah Geldhart, a woman in her mid-twenties, sits reading. She smiles, and nods to herself.

Martin Geldhart, her brother, late-twenties, enters, smiling. He watches her for a moment, unnoticed.

MARTIN: Whenever I walk into this room, I tell you, I expect some *guy*, you know, with a manuscript, to kick me out. Hey, Sarah.

SARAH: Oh, God, hello, Martin. I know. I've always hated this room. Look at all these books.

(Sarah shakes her head, rueful.)

MARTIN: Miss Barzakian just cornered me in reception and told me that last week Ventrice, that poet? Know him? So he's—he chases Dad down the hall and he says, and I repeat . . . "I'll kill you—you dirty-Jew-kike-bastard, I'll kill you, you prick."*(Beat)* It wouldn't be so bad if he were a decent poet.

SARAH: The publishing world, eh? So. What do you think of all this?

MARTIN *(Thinks for a second, simple):* It's a bore. You know? What're you reading?

SARAH: Oh, something Dad's thinking of publishing. It was sitting here. God knows what he—what he's thinking. "Hobson-Jobson. A Glossary of Colloquial Anglo-Indian Words & Phrases." I mean, tell me, Martin, am I out of touch here or will, like, two people buy this?

MARTIN: Well, I mean, please. No wonder, is it, we're going bankrupt?

SARAH: No, but still, I do feel funny being dragged into it, don't you?

MARTIN *(Cheerful):* Well, you *are* a stockholder.

SARAH: Right. I was kind of hoping that by the time I flew in, they'd have it all sorted out. You know? When you're actually happy they've delayed the flight? Anyway, I read the manuscript they're fighting about on the plane and, I mean—

MARTIN: It was bound to come to a head, wasn't it? Look— just take a look at these shelves. You can't do it. You can't go on publishing accounts of—look at this: a two-volume tome on the destruction of the Sephardim during the Spanish Inquisition? Reprints of Traven and Pirandello. Firbank? *That's* big. How many Kreeger/Geldhart books do you see in the stores?

SARAH: Oh please, Martin, do you think we still have bookstores on the coast? Let me tell you, I went into a Crown or Dalton or something. You walk in. It's like a Burger King. There're "blips" from the video games . . . it's like, "Buy a Coke, getta Book." I said to the clerk, "I'm looking for E. E. Cummings." He said, "Self-help, second aisle on the left." And I said, "Are you people still in the *book* business, or what?"

MARTIN: So what'd you think of the manuscript?

SARAH: The thing is, the plane was, there wasn't an empty, and so you can't really focus on the—

MARTIN: You're saying you skimmed? Is that it?

SARAH: Hey, you know I hate to read, it's not fair. But actually it seemed funny. The dirty part, the thing with the two guys.

MARTIN: I hate being dragged into this. And I swore not even to come down here. I sat there after Dad called, you know, I hung up and said to myself, "This is their trip, I'm not part of it. Let them sort it all out because I just don't care."

SARAH: Cut to: Here we are. And . . .

MARTIN: Of course to say "No, sorry, I can't," is not an option.

SARAH: Yeah. *(Beat)* Why *do* we come? I mean, because I'm shooting the show, we're doing three shows back-to-back, and I beg them to rearrange the schedule. Because I've had a summons from Dad. Who said to me, *last* time I was home, "Sarah, how do you actresses remember your lines?" And I go, "What do you mean?" And he said, quite earnestly, "Because none of you are, let's face it now, all that bright, really. Are you?"

MARTIN *(Smiles):* Well, he calls me a "gardener's apprentice," whatever *that* is. At Passover he asked me how the tree-pruning business was. I mean, I teach landscape architecture at Vassar, for Christ's sake. Which is silly, but still. *(Beat, peeved)* They're late.

SARAH: When has Dad ever not kept you waiting? They're in the library with Aaron's novelist. What's his name?

MARTIN: Val Chenard.

SARAH: Val Chenard. It's like the name of a bad restaurant. In Toronto.

MARTIN: Duck, with a pop-tart filling glaze—Val Chenard. *(Beat)* And how is the show?

SARAH: Better than I thought. It's very hip for children's television. A little too hip, I think, sometimes frankly. And everyone is like, way too thrilled. But still. "Safe-Sex-Tips-for-Tots" *is* a good skit. *(Beat)* We didn't really do it—a joke.

MARTIN: Yeah well, no. I saw one. We recently got television in Poughkeepsie. You were a caveman's wife. You were singing "When I'm Sixty-four."

SARAH: Martin, can I ask you something? Does anything happen up there? Are you having a life at all?

MARTIN *(Smiles):* And do you know of anyone now who has any sort of a life? Today? People sit alone at diner

counters eating meat loaf and thinking of mom. No
one has a life.

SARAH: No.

MARTIN: No. I have my orchard, my bonsai. And *they're* fun.

SARAH: Hey, listen. What I have to do is fly right back to
L.A. tonight. I have to turn right back around, but let's
grab dinner, can we? After all this?

MARTIN: I can't. I'm sorry. I have to get back, I—

SARAH: No, I understand. No, no. Don't say a thing—

MARTIN: But, Sarah, hey, it's only that there just won't be
time. Once we get outta here, and then, you know, I'd
miss the ten-twenty, and the next train is like, two-o-
seven or something. And I have to be in Rhinebeck at
dawn 'cause I'm putting up a windbreak on the Hudson with the sophomores, which is fun. I still seem to
get tired, I don't know.

SARAH: Hey, Martin, remember when we were kids, waiting
in this room with some awful thing going on down the
hall. Mom and Dad screaming at each other.

MARTIN: Are you kidding? Who could forget?

SARAH: And we were royalty. There used to be so many people working here.

MARTIN: There were never very many people working here,
sweetie.

SARAH: It seemed like it. Listen, I don't mean to sound like
an idiot, but does bankruptcy actually mean there's a
day when this whole place folds up?

ISAAC *(Entering. Wearing a dark suit of impeccable cut. He
has the slightest of accents—Belgian/German, barely
detectable):* It's not that bad. Aaron exaggerates. Hullo,
sweetheart, I'm glad you came—to get on a plane!

SARAH: Daddy?

ISAAC: You know your brother has his little Stanford-Whar-
ton-Mafia flowcharts he waves in my face and screams.

SARAH: Daddy. What do you think you're doing? *(Picks up a
manuscript from atop the desk)* I mean, "Hobson-Jobson. A Glossary of Colloquial Anglo-Indian Words &
Phrases"?

ISAAC: So what's the big deal? A *dictionary*, do you know

how few people bother to publish 'em anymore? And I'm not talking, please, about the university presses for a tax loss. I've always done a dictionary now and then if it was interesting enough. Hi, Martin. So. You came too, huh? Well. Your brother must've been very pushy with you. You always ignore me when I ask you to come.

MARTIN: Always nice to see you, Dad.

ISAAC: So, tell me, did you get the Edmund Wilson I sent you? I never heard from you. The memoirs.

MARTIN: No, I got it.

SARAH: So what is it? You're not bankrupt, I'm not going to find this place turned into Rug City?

AARON *(Enters. Younger than Martin and dressed more like an ad-exec than publisher):* You don't think you were rude to Val?

MARTIN *(To Aaron):* Hi.

ISAAC: Was I? I don't think so. I was really rather even-keeled, maybe a little blunt, but he virtually spat on the Krasslow manuscript.

AARON *(With absolute relish):* Yes, he did, didn't he? But the Krasslow, Dad, is the last word in boredom. Let me tell you, Val is right. These ossified old academic frauds you trot out every couple of years. You knew Val would be openly contemptuous of your Krasslow, and you deliberately maneuvered him into insulting you.

ISAAC: That's simply paranoid. I'm not that clever.

AARON: Yes, you are. I've seen you do it to me. It's something you do. You navigate a conversation into this place wherein not to insult you would be psychically impossible. Hey, you know something? I don't want to get into a word thing with you, Dad. Do you realize he's about to bugger off to Knopf? And they, Father, let me assure, this'll hit the stores by Wednesday or something. They'll publish it in a second.

ISAAC: Nevertheless.

AARON: And reap a hell of a lot of cashola so doing, damn it!

ISAAC: So what do you think of your brother's little agenda to take over the company?

MARTIN: Oh come on, Isaac, you're not serious.

ISAAC: I've seen it fermenting in him! What do you think, I'm a village idiot?

AARON: Please.

ISAAC: Please! A blood lust for profitmaking. You knew the kind of work we publish—and you have this arrogant idea that you could—God knows the lingo you people use—

AARON: You people? *You people?* What is that supposed to mean?

ISAAC: You know exactly what I mean. You wanna accuse me of bigotry toward MBAs, fine, go ahead. You're not working at Gulf and Western.

AARON: Just this morning, he actually asked me if I wouldn't be happier as a sales rep.

SARAH: Oh dear.

(There is a silence.)

ISAAC: The reason the stock of this company has been kept in the family is because I wished to avoid precisely the kind of confrontation we are having now. If Aaron cannot make peace with the mandate by which *my* company is to be run, he should not be vice-president. No company would settle for less. It is unfortunate, sure, I wanted at least one of you here, but perhaps—

AARON *(Quiet):* That's very clear, yeah. Thanks. But the reason I'm here, you know, is that I actually value the stock I hold in this house. Do you need to be reminded? I own twenty percent of this place, Martin *a quarter*, and Sarah fifteen. And if you continue the course you're on, we will be flattened.

ISAAC: Not necessarily. You don't know that I'm not going to come up with—

AARON: No you won't, and we will be taken over by someone who is in the book business by accident—some real-estate developer dying for a salon, and this town is full of 'em! A lonely guy lookin' for a tax loss, they'll sniff this place out, hey. Simon and Schuster is owned by an oil company, Dad. These people come in, hang new wallpaper and dollar bills before the end of the first day. You're going to leave us with nothing—a dead company.

ISAAC: The Chenard book is crapola, kiddo, there's no denying that.

MARTIN: Actually, I don't think so.

ISAAC: Ahh, you read it. You have a literary opinion, Mr. Johnny-Appleseed-of-the-Hudson here?

AARON: I sent it to both of them.

MARTIN: I finished it on the train coming down here. I think it's powerful. I cried. I don't know why.

ISAAC: You're a gardener, Martin, please.

MARTIN *(Smiles at Sarah):* You can't imagine how much we look forward to seeing you, Isaac. I don't know. It's just the way you make everyone feel so welcome, or . . .

SARAH: And hey, please? What's with this "gardener" business, Dad? Your son's a Rhodes Scholar. You're starting to sound like some sort of Fulton Fishmarket thug, calling names. And besides, what little I read of the book, I sort of liked too.

AARON *(Turns to Martin):* You like the book? You really do? I thought you would. I thought you might, both of you. It's something, isn't it?

ISAAC: Excuse me. I've made up my mind. I don't need a little shit-ass democratic committee here to tell me, please, you got it? *(Pause)* Forgive me for losing my temper, for speaking this way. But I'm gonna publish Louis Fuchold's six volumes on the Nazi medical experiments.

AARON: What? What are you—?

ISAAC *(Calm):* Yes, that's exactly what I'm going to do. That I even let you near a . . . a . . . decision on such a matter is. . . . You think that I am going to publish some trashy novel by a slicko-hipster?

AARON: Dad, this is exactly the problem, this is what I . . . you just decided this? What am I doing here? Just to balance the books?

ISAAC: Abraham Kreeger, your mother's father, started this imprint to publish serious work that was valuable in the larger world. We've played fast and loose with that mandate and made some bucks, and God knows I don't intend to lose any sleep over *that*. I knew how far we had to go in order to grow. But now is the time to get back what we lost. And this Chenard book—is meretricious bullshit! I wanted my time back after I read it.

MARTIN: Well, I think you're misreading it.

ISAAC *(A low growl):* I tend not to misread books. I tend to know exactly the lay of the land.

MARTIN: You have no doubts about your judgment?

ISAAC: Not in regard to this matter.

AARON: Then tell me—why have we been losing so much money?

ISAAC *(Softens, shakes his head):* Something has happened. The way in which people read. Perceive. There used to be some silence to life. There is now none. Just static, white noise, fireworks, and boredom all around you. We lose money because we do something that is no longer held to be vital, we're a side-thought to life. And now here you come, Aaron wanting to save us from destruction, running around here with your manuscript like some kind of Typhoid Mary. *(Isaac looks at the manuscript)* You come to me here with bright-lights-little-people, less-than-nothing, Tammy Yannovitch—a *hydra*—she's not a writer, she's a monster out of ancient Greece come to swallow cultures, lives, whole cities. These kids with eyes like pinwheels, typing out their little baubles of syntax. *This ain't literature. It's a dress.* You don't read this book. You get a nice little, strung-out, anorexic model who doesn't need a lot of covering, and you put it on her to wear to a gallery opening. *(Beat)* So listen, Aaron, what I'm saying to you is—it's simple—you've never burdened anyone with your editorial ambitions until now. You're doing fine. You've learned a lot. But these are very tricky waters out there. Forget about this. Go back to your ledgers and you'll be fine. Leave the heavy stuff to me, okay?

AARON: You begged me to come into this business. I mean, these two had sense enough to run a million miles. Now you're trying to kill it off. I can't just sit back and—

SARAH: Listen. Please. It's just books. Really. Please. I see this behavior and I know what's up. You feel usurped.

ISAAC: No, sweetie, please, uh-uh, no.

SARAH: Oh yes, no, you feel "threatened." De-balled by your son.

ISAAC: Sweetheart, that's terrific but please, none of your Neighborhood Playhouse psychologizing. I published Wilhelm Fliess, while you were at tap class learning shuffle-ball-flap. "Threatened."

AARON: Hey, you know, I'm not gonna argue that this is not a trashy world out there. I mean, come on, but so what?

MARTIN: Aaron tells me if you go ahead and publish the Fuchold Nazi medical experiment book, you won't be able to handle anything else on the spring list except for a couple of the old reprints. Is that right?

ISAAC: The Nazi is six volumes. I can't hold off production. He's been working for thirty-four years. The man practically, he comes to editorial meetings in his casket. We've never been a big house, so now for a while maybe we're a little smaller. It's not a matter of bankruptcy. It's scale. I'll take a reduction in—

AARON: That's really great. You'll take a cut? Have you seen your Visa bills? For a man who has such rigorous standards—

ISAAC (Dangerous and insistent): Don't! Don't you dare to presume to tell me what to spend, nobody—nobody has ever told me what to do. Not your mother, not the banks, and most certainly not my accountant son. (Beat) Listen. Why are you so certain the Fuchold will not be read anyhow? Do you know something I don't?

MARTIN (Gentle, reasonable): Maybe you're not wrong. But why not let Aaron run with this. What harm can it do?

ISAAC: A lot, a lot, it can all slip away, in ways you can't imagine, everything.

(There is a silence in which Isaac seems to disappear into himself.)

MARTIN (Reluctant): The thing is, we've all noticed—you're becoming unapproachable. And it's like you're on some sort of end-run to self-destruct. We don't know what to do. Do you like to know—there's a whole hell of a lot of phone-action. The topic? *(He gestures at Isaac)* And it's not unwarranted, it's a *bore*, but it's *not* unwarranted. You worry us. No end. Look at what you've been publishing. That Englishman's book, Jonally— *The Failure of Art and the Triumph of Technology*? A swipe here at Diaghilev and Stravinsky, a sneer at the Bauhaus, and why not knock off abstract expressionism while you're at it just for a laugh? *(Beat)* I mean it's time for another tack, Pop, 'cause you're starting to come off as some sort of neo-con.

ISAAC *(Picks up manuscript):* Uh-hum, sure, a neo-con, well, may I, I'll just read you a little passage here. *(He pauses to make sure they're with him)* "Alter leaned against the bar, mouth open in recollection of those black hands on his jeans. The feeling of release and submission that comes when someone else unsnaps the buttons—and then, the intrusive rightness of the kid's lips on him, surrounding him in the alley—the cold—the heat—and wetness as his shirt is lifted up towards the spire of the Chrysler building, glowing above them" . . . etc., etc.

(He looks at Martin, triumphant.)

SARAH: Well, Dad, I don't understand. What's the big deal here? We all know about blow jobs, don't we?

ISAAC: Yes, we know about blow jobs. That's hardly the . . .

SARAH: Well then maybe you publish all these politico books because there's no sex in them? They're totally flaccid. See, Dad, you just need to get out more is all.

MARTIN: The thing of it is, Dad, you see, I promised Aaron that if I liked the book, I'd support him. Whatever that meant. Understand? I do like the book. Aaron is your partner. You drew him in, made promises. And you are able to be the fairest man I know. Occasionally. So publish the book and what's the big deal? Come on.

ISAAC: What do you think, I'll be cornered? I'll be dictated to? *(He looks around the room)* What the hell is going on here? *What?*

AARON: I'm sorry, Dad. I don't understand the Nazi obsession. It has silenced me. I mean, what do you say to it? Look at the spring and fall lists last year. *(Beat) An Atlas of the Holocaust.* Maps. Blueprints. I. G. Farben's structural reports. All of it on acid-free paper with a hand-sewn binding, a Japanese printing, wholesaling at one twenty-nine ninety-five? *(Beat)* You take the bread out of our mouths. It's heartbreaking to say how much we lost on that. And please. I won't even discuss the losses on *Water on Fire, an Oral History of the Children of Hiroshima.*

SARAH: Hey. It's just books. You know? I see what's happening here. You'll all use these issues as leverage, whatever the cost. Hey, I know what I'm talking about. Listen, I talk to other actors, and it's so fucking dull. It's just this crushing bore—they're all dying from their dogmas. What they will or will not do, and it's a total snooze. Who cares? It doesn't matter. It just doesn't make a difference.

ISAAC: No, it does matter. It does make a difference. They should care. Otherwise, you end up? What? Heinrich Mann doing little drawings at his desk at Warners. Kazan in a cold sweat, saying yes to anything. All the little failures of spirit—they add up and they add up badly. But, of course, that's the American seduction, right? Not a thing matters here, it's all disposable. Forget your history, forget what you believed in, forget your fire. Forget your fire. *(Beat)* You leave your fire at the door these days, right? You see, Sarah, it matters very much what I choose to fight for. *(Beat)* So, Aaron. Let me ask you, from a literary standpoint, not a commercial one, why should I publish *Rising Tide?*

AARON *(Laughs slightly, closes his eyes):* No. Please. Hey, I'm not that dumb.

SARAH: Well, it's true, honey, you've given, you know, all these terribly mercantile reasons and all, but no literary—

AARON: Yeah, well, don't count on my weakness as a critical thinker, Dad. I'm hip to you. One by one, point by point, I could say, "Oh, the book deals in themes of blah-blah-blah." And you would say, "Oh, no, it doesn't. If *that's* what you think the book deals in, you're wrong. A book that *does* deal in blah-blah-blah, I would be very interested in publishing. But this book here doesn't, son. Sorry. Find me a nice German novel about a village in '34 to have translated."

ISAAC: Do me at least the favor of not telling me what I would say to you if you presented to me an argument I haven't heard.

AARON: No. Of course. *(Beat. He smiles)* No, I'm not much of a reader, we know. I'm more comfortable, you tell me, with the balance sheet and the projections. The numbers don't lie. All that. *(Pause)* And all done with a smirk, as if you've always held the opinion that making a lot of money was somehow vulgar. For a publisher. *(Beat)* I just don't get it. Are your literary opinions so profoundly held that they hold to the point where your children have to halt you? Is this ceaseless drive to run us into the ground circling any particular point, Dad, or is it just that in the six years since Mother died, you've become suicidal? Because you're way too smart to stand on ceremony over Anthony-fucking-Trollope. *(Beat)* I *think*.

ISAAC: This, Aaron, is simply beneath contempt. This line of reasoning, it's gutter reasoning, kiddo, and—

AARON: Maybe, but ever since your wife died, if we had a graph curve it would look like the north face of Everest from '81 on.

ISAAC: I wouldn't confuse high standards with missing your mother.

AARON: Yeah, well, the thing is, I don't think this has anything to do with "standards." What I think is that you are a man who has lost his sense of humor.

ISAAC: My *what*?

AARON: You've lost your sense of humor. What happened to the low joke? The frivolous gesture? Bawdiness? You have no time for a laugh. That's why you should publish this book. That's my best argument.

ISAAC: Excuse me, let me get this straight here. I've lost my sense of humor and if I publish the Val Chenard book, I'll get it back? What're you? Nuts?

MARTIN: It's true, Dad, you've become this Cotton Mather type. You're gonna drop dead from rigor any day now. It's true, Sarah, tell him.

SARAH: Hey, I don't know what to say. I see you smirking, Martin, and I hate this. And besides, what do I know about it? I sing songs to eight-year-olds about trichinosis. I shouldn't even be here. But it's true, Daddy, you get more and more intractable, more isolated in your positions.

AARON: You don't go out. You don't see anyone, you sit around with your illustrated letters, your collection of first editions, signed postcards, sneaking off to auctions—

ISAAC: Please, please, this is—

AARON: He bought a postcard of Adolph Hitler's. A little drawing.

ISAAC: Enough.

AARON: Well, what is that *about*?

MARTIN: A postcard of Hitler's?

ISAAC: He painted, you know that, as a boy. I mean, once he was a boy. He sent a postcard on which he had painted a little watercolor of a church. He painted mostly churches. Landmarks in old Vienna. It had a fascination for me. Done in 1916. It wasn't cheap, but it triggered something. I don't know. A view of a world. I am out of step with myself lately, here in New York. I am out of step with myself.

MARTIN: I understand all that, but I don't understand why that precludes publishing Aaron's book. It's a comic novel. A little book. You just can't give everything equal weight, equal moral weight—

ISAAC: Maybe you can. Maybe you should. Maybe that's exactly the problem.

MARTIN: No. I don't think so. For you, rejecting this book becomes this—affirmation—of how you're supposed to live your life, saying "no" to everything. Let me ask you this: You've become a pretty good publisher of books about horror. It's all death camps and napalm and atrocities with you.

ISAAC: Martin—

MARTIN: The question is—just because you've started to deal in historical hardware, do you imagine that makes you above some sort of reproach? It's "Oh, we can't criticize Isaac Geldhart, we've gotta take him dead serious. After all, he published *Hazlitt on Cannibalism*." Well, to my mind, all that makes you is a very cautious academic pornographer, a sensationalist with Sulka ties. "See the bodies pile up, watch the dead, see how bad everything is. Why bother engaging?"

ISAAC: This is rich coming from you who has deliberately shut himself away from all interaction up there in Poughkeepsie. You, with your seed-hybrids. Humorless? No, I don't think so. I am just so afraid of this trash piling up around us. I am afraid of the young. *You.* Let me tell you—I am. "Publish this book 'cause you're not funny anymore." My God, I prefer at least your arguments about fiscal doom, but spare me that playing-to-the-balcony crap about missing your mom. I am destroying this company because life is not worth living without your mother? Let me tell you, that wasn't the greatest marriage in the world. I don't think about her a lot these days. So phooey to that approach— stick to the numbers, Aaron.

SARAH *(Cuts him off—furious):* Who do you think you're talking about? That's my mother you're talking about. Please! What the hell is the matter with you? Do you hear yourself? Aaron's trying to help. But all I can see is you treating people badly. Treating Aaron with this superior bullying contempt.

AARON: No, hey, it's what I signed on for. You get used to it. It's like you can insult anyone as long as it's done sort of elegantly.

ISAAC: Who? I do this? I really do this? But think about what you're asking me to do. You want me to change the direction of this company. To do so will drive me mad. I don't even know how to. You've gotta bear with me a little. So what if I'm humorless? Surely that's not a valid reason for taking over my life's work? I would say that a sense of humor is nice, but really, in the end, beside the point.

MARTIN: Maybe. I hope not. When was the last time we had dinner together, Pop?

ISAAC: I always ask, but you turn me down cold, so I don't ask anymore. Don't blame me for that. I made an effort to remain close but—

MARTIN: Yes, sure. On terms that are unliveable.

(He lights a smoke.)

ISAAC: I know. I'm tough in a restaurant, but I—what is this *smoking* business? What are you doing *smoking*? You have no business smoking, Martin.

MARTIN: Your obsession over the martini, for instance. Only a miserable man could require such precision in his drink. The little ice container that has to be three-quarters filled to keep the extra martini perfectly cold. The "problem" with the twist. You actually, I sat there—you said to the waiter, "There's a problem with the twist." You actually—I mean, it used to be funny. But grimly gnawing and hacking away at your salmon—sending it back—you sent it back *three times.*

ISAAC *(With a contemptuous shrug):* It wasn't right.

MARTIN: Yeah, well, the maitre'd practically stabbed you. I would have applauded. That was the last time we had dinner together.

ISAAC: I thought we had a nice time, Martin.

MARTIN: It was like dinner with Duvalier. Both of them.

AARON: Dad, do you remember when we had a best seller? It was seven years ago. And it kept us alive. This book can go the same way. Can't you just simply trust me—once? Just now—once.

(Pause.)

ISAAC: No. Not on this. No.

MARTIN: Then I'll sign over my shares of this company to Aaron. He'd be the majority stockholder. I don't want to do that to you, but believe me, I will. Because Mom left us those shares to do what we pleased with. So why push it?

SARAH: Hey, hold on, Martin, what are you doing? Come on, are you kidding here?

ISAAC: Oh, so that's where we are. So how did it go, Aaron? You called up your brother and made him an offer? That is what you learned at Wharton? Bought you a nice degree, didn't I?

SARAH: Listen, Aaron. This is not just some faceless takeover. Martin. People don't recover. Families, they just fold up, you know? Never to speak again. Are we like that? That sort of family? Over money? You've got to find some way to compromise. All of you. Because this is just horseshit.

ISAAC: I sense your little sister would not be in on your takeover. So, Sarah, darling?

AARON: You cannot possibly win this one, Dad. There's just no way.

SARAH: Hold it. Why don't you bother asking me? I'm not going to sit here like some dumb—nobody bothers asking me what I think. "What does she think?" *(Beat)* What I think is this. I don't want to turn this into some sort of horrible little . . . *thing.* But, Martin, if you hand your stocks to Aaron, then I'll hand mine over to Dad. *(Shrugs, shakes her head)* Well, sorry. But nobody bothers asking me what I think.

AARON: Sarah.

MARTIN: Hey, you know, Sarah, it might not be such a bad idea to let this thing run its course.

SARAH: Why? Because you're enjoying yourself?

ISAAC: So, there you have it. This is, I think, a stalemate.

AARON: Sarah, what are you doing?

ISAAC: Think now, Aaron, didn't Wharton provide you with the next step?

(Silence.)

Why don't you take some time to think it over?

AARON: I have Val in the library. He'll be outta here. He's not just gonna . . .

ISAAC: Well, I will ask him to wait. You talk this over without me. My position is clear. I will *not* compromise. I will not be manipulated. But I am not sure that you should either.

(He exits. Silence in his wake.)

SARAH: God, he is a tricky bastard.

AARON: Oh, yes?

MARTIN: I need, I think, a drink about now.

AARON: I mean, the idea of you selling your stock to Dad—
and, by the way, what's he going to pay you with?
Some first editions? Terrific. His collection of illustrated letters? He just went into hock on that Hitler
postcard. You want that on your wall?

SARAH: He hung it up?

AARON: Look, there's no cash. We're on empty here.

SARAH: He needs to see a negotiable way out. Bend a little,
he'll bend too.

AARON: It's way past that. He got you to offer him your
stock. The man'll have fifty-five percent, just what he's
after. And if you do that, ultimately, you'll be killing
him.

SARAH: But wouldn't taking control from him do him in just
as surely—and a hell of a lot more viciously? Have you
ever thought that you're acting out of sheer anger
towards him? Nothing to do with saving the company?
Just rage?

AARON: And if I am? So? What if you're giving into him out
of some need to be loved? That's not just as bad?

SARAH: Hey—

AARON: Get ready for next season—*Lullabies from the War-
saw Ghetto.* On every remainder shelf in the country.

MARTIN: I'm going to have a drink. This is exhausting.

(He exits.)

AARON: Martin!—

SARAH: Why is he smoking and drinking all over the place?
What's with him? When did he start? He knows he's
supposed to be careful.

AARON: I don't know. I've never been able to read anyone in
this family, so don't ask me. *(Beat)* What do I do now?
'Cause I guess I actually seem to have finally blown it
here.

SARAH: I'm sorry, Aaron.

AARON: Well, I just have to find a way to think of this as a positive.

SARAH: Aaron, I'm trying to do the right thing, to do the most right thing.

AARON: No, you're trying to do exactly what I did. You're trying to get his approval. *(Beat)* I had this idiot notion that he and I'd sit here at this table talking about books. And really he has—not once solicited my opinion, not once asked me what I was reading, over a cup of coffee, which is all I wanted.

SARAH: I know. Listen, I'm so dumb I fly across the country because he asks me to. I—look at me—dress like a refugee from *Little Women.* I think of important issues to—I actually sat on the plane tearing through back issues of the *New Republic* and *The Nation*, trying to find witty things to knock him dead with. And last month, he sent a bunch of S. J. Perelman first editions. Why? No note. Nothing. But I sit there for hours thinking, "What's he trying to tell me? Be funnier?" I mean, really.

AARON: Last week, someone asked him what you were up to. He told them you were a clown for hire for children's birthday parties. This, after he saw you on the UNICEF anniversary show. Looked at the TV and mumbled, "Americans," as if you were a foreigner.

SARAH: A birthday clown. That's terrific. I love it.

AARON: Yeah, well, he introduced me at the ABA as his bookkeeper, so you're not alone. *(Beat)* Look. Seeing as this is pretty much over, we should, at least, be able to have a meal together. Brooklyn. "Garjulos"? The puttanesca is still like blood.

SARAH: Oh, shit, Aaron, I can't. Really, I have to catch the nine o'clock to the coast. We're doing "K" tomorrow.

AARON: "K"?

SARAH: The letter "K", yeah. It's my letter.

AARON: Oh. May I ask you this? Are you still involved with your producer? Is that still on?

SARAH: Why? I mean?

AARON: I'm just curious. It was an issue for you last time I saw you. "This older man." That's still happening?

SARAH: "Happening" implies action, you know? Motion. I just sit around waiting for the guy, repeating lines to myself that would send a sane person running a million miles. Like, "Oh, he's leaving his wife of fifteen years. It was over anyway." So mostly, I wait. *(Beat)* And yes, fine, he goes days without calling.

AARON: But you settle for that? An older man pushing you, doling out little bits here and there—?

SARAH: No, I admit it, you don't have to press the goddamn point. He's absolutely the cliche of a father fixation.

AARON: Well, just last week, our father accused me of being a person most free within a cliche. He said I was liberated by banality, so. That is that?

SARAH: What're you going to do?

AARON: What can I do? I'm gonna back down, and help steer us through bankruptcy. It's okay—this thing was doomed from the beginning, from the start. I went out with Chenard in college.

SARAH: With?—Oh God, Aaron, honey. Is that why the book has been so—

AARON: No. The book is good. This is not a clouded issue.

SARAH: I didn't know, Aaron. I knew that you were . . . but I mean, I just didn't know. You've been so silent.

AARON: No, well, yes. It was a thing. We used to have things. Everybody had a little "thing." Judy doesn't know. Nobody. He liked me because I admitted I knew nothing about literature, only about maybe making a profit in the service of art. He thought I was actually totally naïve. Which, of course, I was. *(Beat)* We have dinner. The people we went to school with are off, you know, doing bad performance art in Hoboken, or in closed sessions with the SEC over insider jobs downtown. Nothing in between. I'm in publishing. We have this link.

SARAH: So this has been with you?

AARON: And I am almost totally domesticated. Judy bought me these slippers from Brooks Brothers. With lamb's wool. I looked at them and thought, "Shackles, goddamn it. How do I end up here?"

SARAH: I am sorry, Aaron. That's hard. I know. That's really hard.

AARON: No. It was pathetic to have thought of this as my big chance. To prove to Dad—I mean, I must think like a seven-year-old.

SARAH: Well, I'm still a toddler, so at least you're ahead of me.

AARON: Too bad we couldn't have a bite.

SARAH: Yeah, well, I've gotta get back. I have the letter "K" to take care of. Such as it is.

AARON: And a father fixation to nurture, right?

(Martin enters with a drink in hand.)

MARTIN: Dad is sitting in the library with your writer, Aaron.

AARON: What's he doing?

MARTIN: His "Decline of the West, Part Three" speech. Chenard is laughing.

AARON: Look, Sarah, if you were to back *us*, the very worst is that Dad will have been wrong. Well, he should be able to learn to live with that. It's not the end of the world. He'll simply have been mistaken, and I'll have helped him—*we'll* have helped him. Come on.

SARAH: Look, maybe we should all just pull back. When he comes in, we'll try and start this from scratch. Just reason it out, okay?

MARTIN: I'm not pulling back. Hey, it's Aaron's. I'm out, and I don't give a fuck what you publish really.

SARAH: Hey, come on Martin. Please. What are you talking about?

MARTIN: We go months without speaking to one another. We're all afraid of each other—slightly put off. There's some sort of competitiveness under the surface, and I've never cared for it. We're better off keeping away from each other. And more than that, let me tell you— I am above this struggle.

ISAAC *(Entering):* So, it's getting late. We all have places to go, and I'm tired. How do you want to handle this?

MARTIN: Publish *Hustler* or publish Proust. I don't want to have anything to do with it anymore. Your books. God. I am so tired of these books. And your endless posturing, position-taking, ranting, judging. The only thing I miss is Mom. She wouldn't put up with any of this crap for a second. She'd know what to do. Damn it. I just—coming down here is too much. It's done me in. I miss Mom.

ISAAC: The only part I believe is the last. Such poison. Martin, why such poison, always?

MARTIN: Poison! You want to talk about poison? Look at what you've done. You've created a family of literary zombies. You know that people are afraid of you. It's why you've gotten so far. Yes. "Isaac Geldhart knows something, he came from some awful childhood in Europe that nobody knows about." He has a "seer-like standing in the book world." Blah-blah-blah—phooey. Let me tell you, we're fucked up by it. I grew up running around this building. When I was eight, you gave me the *Iliad* in Greek so that someday I could read it. Monster! People's lives are ruined by books and they're all you know how to relate to, Dad. You too, Aaron, for all your talk. You too, Sarah, pretending you hate to read. Sometimes I want to take a pruning shears and do an Oedipus on myself. I counted my books last week. Do you know how many I have? Want to take a guess?

(No one says anything.)

Fourteen thousand, three hundred, and eighty-six. The sixty crates of books that Mom left me. Well, I finally had them carted up the Hudson, but I had to have shelves built. The whole house. Every room. And instead of just guessing—I was, I mean—speechless. A wreck of a life. It just flashed before my eyes. No sex, no people, just books 'til I die. Dickens. In *French*. The bastard didn't write in French. What the fuck am I doing with *Dombey and Son* in French? The twelve-volume *Conquest of Mexico*. Two hundred cookbooks. The *Oxford World Classics*, the little ones with the blue bindings, you know?

ISAAC: You got those?

MARTIN: They're all just words. And this is life, and besides, I hear the book chains are now selling preemptive strike video games, so why bother anyway? I'm out.

ISAAC: But really, darling, there are limits.

MARTIN: Yes. That's exactly right. There are limits. I believe I know that. Hey, I spent most of my sixteenth year getting chemotherapy, remember? And it's not that long ago, I can still feel it. I cannot waste my life. I feel you people dragging me into this thing. You want this confrontation, Dad. You want nothing more than your children gathered around you, fighting. Well forget it. You don't know what I feel in my back, in my bones. I wake up some days and I'm crying. I think I'm still at Sloan-Kettering, lying there hairless and white and filling up with glucose from a drip. Hey! I can't get that time back. I feel all the needles, some days, my lymph nodes, and I'm sweating. And part of my life is spent in fear, waiting. I know none of us has forever, know that very well, and I care very much how I spend my time. And involved in an internecine war over a publishing house, is, by my reckoning, Father, a dead waste. *And* if I choose to live with plants as an assistant lecturer at an overrated Seven Sisters school, *that* is my goddamn choice. But let's clear up something finally: I am not a goddamn gardener, and you are never going to goad me back into this life by calling me one. And Sarah is not a clown at children's birthday parties, Dad, and Aaron isn't a fucking accountant. You are really charming about your superiority, Dad. But you're really alone, too. This Nazi book jag of yours— it scares me.

(Long pause.)

ISAAC: I spent a couple of days, a little boy, wandering around after the liberation. I saw a particular kind of man—a wraith-like figure—who could only have been in the camps. But with a brown pinstripe suit, a fleur-de-lis on his tie and manicured nails, trying to pick up where he left off, as if you could. I never say anthing about this. Why talk? Why bother? I wasn't in the camps.

You know? They're busy throwing the Farbers and the Hirsches into the ovens, and I'm happily eating smoked eels in the basement, with my Stendahl, my Dumas. What did I know? I was protected, sheltered by my cousins. And then I got out of the basement and into the wrecked world. I came to this country. You reinvent yourself. Make it as a bon vivant in Manhattan. Meet this woman—this extraordinary woman. Marry. Have these kids. Go to so many cocktail parties, host so many more, but still they . . . haunt. *(Beat)* I have kept my eyes closed to the world outside the basement for so long. The wrecked world all around us. But I can no longer close my eyes. *(He turns to Aaron)* My son. You are fired. I will give you a week to clear your desk, and I will give you letters of recommendation. But I will not speak to you, I will not communicate with you, I will not . . . *(Pause)* . . . *give at all.* Kiddo. To the victor go the spoils.

SARAH: Wait a second, wait a second. I see what you're doing. You want to use *me* to screw Aaron. And you think I would go along with that? You think that's the kind of person I am? That I'd just sit still and watch you? Why—because I feel sorry for you because you weren't in a camp?

ISAAC: Sarah—

SARAH: No. I am going to hand my shares to Aaron. Because you just don't understand. You don't know how to love.

AARON: Wait a second. Let's be clear about this. You just handed me control of this company.

SARAH: Yes. I did.

AARON: You did this to yourself. It didn't have to happen.

ISAAC: Do what you must.

AARON *(Quietly furious):* I warned you. I explained it to you. But you ignore all the signs. You just proceed self-destructively, asking for help, asking to be usurped, upended, damn it. Do you want to hate me? *(Beat)* Well, go ahead. Hate me. But we need cash. I have had an offer. Japanese. And you will no longer run the company, you will be kicked onto the board. I have tried to warn you. But with Martin and Sarah's stock—

with control in my hands, I have no choice. We will be backed by some men in Tokyo who won't give a fuck whether I publish Val Chenard or *Racing Forum* so long as it turns a buck in their direction. And you knew this was coming. You knew it could only end up like this. Well, at least you'll be taken care of. You won't starve to death. I'm sorry. I simply have no choice.

ISAAC: You understand, Aaron, sweetheart. You will just be part of the big pile, the big carcinogenic pile of trash, building up all around you, while life itself no longer seems real.

AARON: Yeah, well, you know, that's not my problem. That's *your* problem, Dad. It's not my fault that life does seem real to me, and I can make peace with that. I don't have a holocaust to pin on my chest. I have my family. My city. Some continuity. The way I think. My friends. I don't want to set life back to its beginnings, and I'm not burdened by thinking I'm one of the world's great thinkers, either. All I can do with the "carcinogenic pile of trash" is sift through it. That's all anyone can do. But my life does seem totally real to me. I do not need to suffer in order to feel alive, Pop. I'm sorry. I'm going to have dinner with my author.

ISAAC *(As Aaron starts out):* Aaron. I hope it works out for you.

(Aaron exits. Isaac crosses to the window, looks out.)

This city. When I got off the boat, I said, "It's going to be so good now, this life, it's all going to be so full." It was snowing.

SARAH: I'm sorry. I have a plane to catch. Daddy . . .

(She exists.)

MARTIN: Dad, why don't we get some dinner? We could take the car. It never gets used. Go across the bridge.

ISAAC: That is not possible.

(He turns to the window. Martin sits down. The lights fade.)

ACT TWO

Three and a half years later. An old apartment in Gramercy Park. Isaac is sitting in a chair, staring out the window. A fierce winter snowstorm swirls around and down over the park. The radio plays, and the radiator hisses steam, gurgles, protests, coughs. The apartment is not so much a home as it is an archive. Floor to ceiling—the room is dominated by books. Though there are also gaping holes, gaps on the shelves where volumes are missing. There are also framed letters—all of which are embellished with drawings. Isaac has a frayed, fogged-in air about him. The door buzzer rings. Isaac sighs, turns off the radio. He puts on his tie and shoes, and is getting on his jacket as Martin enters—layered in snow, parka, scarf, gloves and boots. He stands for a moment, catching his breath.

MARTIN *(Putting his coat, etc., on a hook in the hall):* Didn't you hear the buzzer?

ISAAC *(Eager):* You want tea? Is it cold? It looks a little cold outside?

MARTIN: I had to stand there, struggling with these keys in the ice and the . . . *(Pause. He sighs)* How are you?

ISAAC *(Shrugs):* Who the hell knows, you know? I didn't think you'd get in. I hear on WNYC the trains are backed up to Lake Placid.

MARTIN: No, I came in last night, I—

ISAAC: I see. I see. I see. Last night. You . . . ?

MARTIN: Stayed at a friend's.

(Isaac nods, not thrilled.)

You ate?

ISAAC *(Not interested):* Maybe with the snow, the girl won't come.

MARTIN: The cleaning girl?

ISAAC: This place is—who can live this way? *(Yells suddenly)*

Goddamn it! Who? The kitchen is—have you ever tried to steam a squash? It's a room full of yellow pulp.

MARTIN *(Smiles):* Please.

ISAAC *(Resigned):* Martin, I'm telling you, you can't run a place this big with only a woman who comes in once a week from Belize. The dust, it's like a nuclear winter in this place. *(Runs out of steam)* You have to take three showers a day.

MARTIN: Dad. The social worker. That's today. You remember?

ISAAC: No, no, no. What do you think, I'm an idiot? Today is the maid and the Sotheby lady.

MARTIN *(Quiet):* It's the psychiatric social worker. You agreed. I came into town because you asked me—

ISAAC *(Yelling):* Do I look to you like a man who hasn't got a calendar? Thursday is the social. Today is Tuesday, the cleaning. Please!

MARTIN: Today, actually, Isaac, *is*, in point of fact, Thursday.

(There is silence.)

ISAAC: Without Miss Barzakian how'm I supposed to know my appointments? Idiotic. To have even consented to this.

MARTIN: It would help if you could remember the days of the week.

ISAAC: What for? Just a slab of days, this. Tell me something, Martin, what do you do? You go back to Aaron? With reports?

MARTIN: Yes. He asks.

ISAAC: He asks? And you tell him, "He's doddering, he's slobbering, he's mortifying, the kitchen is a horror? He can't tie his shoes." That sort of thing? Because frankly, if that's the case, I'm better off—

MARTIN *(Suddenly suspicious):* What do you mean the "Sotheby Lady"—what were you talking about before?

ISAAC: I didn't say anything, I didn't say—

MARTIN: What did you do? Have you been trying to get rid of more stuff?

ISAAC: Musselblat the attorney tells me if I can raise enough,

I should be able to make a reasonable offer to get back the company, so—

MARTIN *(Disgusted and exhausted):* Oh, Jesus, Dad. Isaac. What's the matter with you?

ISAAC: I've gotta try, don't I?

MARTIN: We're in Chapter 11. What do you think you can do? It would take a superhuman effort, and you're not in any shape . . .

ISAAC: What do you know about business? What have you ever known about business? Please. Please. *(Takes a moment)* You know, Martin, yesterday, I saw the most magnificent pair of shoes on Irving Place on a young guy, and he had to have someone makin' 'em, I tell ya, 'cause there ain't no guy in this hellhole of a town who can do that particular suede—in one *piece*—I tell you. Probably he was English, and I followed him. I'd buy 'em, even if they were the wrong size. You get a guy to copy 'em, there you are. *(He looks bitterly at his son)* I'll tell you something. I can waste my day in so many goddamn ways, I tell you.

(They both just sit for a moment.)

MARTIN: Dad, have you been for a walk? The park is white. Maybe if it stops snowing.

ISAAC: Do we have to talk? To sit here talking with you—it's like talking to strangers. I really, these little trips in from the country of yours. I don't need 'em, I really don't. I can handle the Sotheby people just fine.

MARTIN: It's the social worker, and it wasn't my idea.

ISAAC *(Scornful):* No, of course not. But if Aaron says I'm incompetent, there's gotta be something to it, right? After all, he sure did such a good job with the company, didn't he?

MARTIN: Nobody is saying anything about your being incompetent—

ISAAC *(Explodes):* Please! Remember who you're talking to! My God, the impertinence!

(Isaac crosses away from Martin. Martin looks at a pile of bills.)

MARTIN: But why didn't you pay the phone people? It's past due. Can't you see this only serves to substantiate—
ISAAC: It's a maelstrom of papers. Who can keep track of them all? Maybe if they were at least in different colors.

(He sees Martin looking at some empty book shelves.)

I have to sell it all. Besides, the disability is up any day now. That's a big check every month to do without. What am I supposed to do?
MARTIN: You sold the old Everyman Encyclopedias?
ISAAC: I got nothing for it. You know what I had to do? I had to go see those pricks at Gotham. I had to walk in the door like some kind of huckster, like it's a grapefruit. I wish your brother'd seen it. *(He looks at Martin)* Tell me something, why do you dress like you're some sort of Paul Bunyan character? It's unbecoming.
MARTIN: I'm sorry. I'll wear a suit next time.

(Silence.)

ISAAC: What do you hear from your sister?
MARTIN: That you still hang up the phone on her.
ISAAC: I'd like to get the hell out of this town. A building blew up just across the park. Apparently there was a cloud of asbestos and now there's cancer for everyone. A janitor was parboiled. The whole street was a freak show.
MARTIN: No, I know. We've talked about this.
ISAAC: Of course, the management company on this property, I think I last saw them in '59, when we signed the papers, and—

(There is a buzz. Martin crosses to the hall for the intercom.)

MARTIN *(Into intercom):* Hello?
ISAAC: They can't hear you. It doesn't work. You can only buzz, not talk, so if, per chance, it happens to be a mugger, well, you're fine.
MARTIN *(Into intercom):* Hello?
MARGE HACKETT *(Over intercom):* It's Marge Hackett.

ISAAC: Occasionally, it works.

MARTIN: Come up to three. *(Pushes the button)* Dad, can I give you some advice?

(Isaac says nothing.)

Just try and answer yes or no. You don't have to—you don't have to do the Isaac Geldhart show. It's not required. They don't let you off on charm. They don't even get it, these people, and if you—

ISAAC: No, I get it. Quit your carping, would you? Making me ill. Standing here giving instructions like I'm your photosynthesis class or something.

(A knock is heard. Isaac exits.)

MARTIN: Dad, she's here.

(Marge Hackett enters. A woman in her fifties— maybe, hard to be sure.)

Hi. We talked on the phone, we spoke. Martin Geldhart.

MARGE: Oh, yes, right. Sure.

MARTIN: I didn't know if you'd make it here.

MARGE: The snow doesn't bother me. I don't mind it.

MARTIN *(Shakes his head, looks at her):* Listen. I know you came all the way here, but I don't think this is the greatest time.

MARGE: On the phone, you said there are bad days.

MARTIN: I would say this appears to be one of them.

MARGE: The depression? It's also, the weather doesn't help much. It can do people in.

MARTIN: Maybe you should come back.

MARGE: Well, I'm here. And your brother . . . ?

MARTIN: Aaron?

MARGE: Was very insistent. Look. The Department is swamped. To get these appointments, and then to get someone to come to the house, it's tough. Why drag it on?

MARTIN *(Resigned):* Okay. *(Beat)* He yells. He was always a bit of a yeller, but now—

MARGE: I am used to it. I don't—it doesn't scare me. But I have to call in. Is there a phone anywhere I can use?

MARTIN: The kitchen. *(He points)* Miss Hackett, I just want you to know—I think this whole business is a big mistake.

(Isaac enters.)

MARGE: Noted.

(She exits.)

MARTIN: She's calling her office. I'll leave you alone.

(Isaac says nothing.)

Please don't stand here yelling at her. Would you? Don't do a number on her. *(Pause. No response)* When she comes in, I'm going to leave you alone.

ISAAC: What? You think I need you to sit here in the room with me?

(Martin starts to leave.)

Martin, how's my tie?

(Marge enters.)

MARTIN: It's fine.

(He exits.)

MARGE: Your phone, it doesn't seem to be working, it's out.

ISAAC: The weather. But you found it?

MARGE: I did find it.

ISAAC: Because sometimes I misplace it. It never rings. *(Beat)* Isaac Geldhart.

MARGE: Yes. Marge Hackett.

ISAAC: Listen to that—"It never rings." Already that sounds like special pleading.

MARGE: Not necessarily.

ISAAC: Actually, to tell you the truth, what it is, is a *relief*. I spent so many years waiting for phones to ring, sitting about, so now . . .

MARGE: The silence is welcome. I understand.

ISAAC: Have we met before? You look . . . no. Did the woman offer you a coffee?

MARGE: I didn't see anyone.

ISAAC: It's Tuesday.

MARGE: No. It's not Tuesday.

ISAAC: No, it's *Thursday*. She has a tendency not to show. Also, she ain't listed, so I'm fucked. *(Pause)* Forgive me. I'm trying to be competent. That's the thing you need to know, is it not?

MARGE: Mr. Geldhart, nothing is being determined here.

ISAAC: Oh, forgive me, I thought something *was* being determined.

MARGE: No. This is a process. No one person can make a dispensation, come to a conclusion.

ISAAC: No one person? There's more of you to come? A tribunal?

MARGE: It's not that bad.

(Isaac looks at the disarray around.)

ISAAC: There is a mess. You should watch out, because there was asbestos across the park. I'm sure it drifted over. I try not to breathe, which is a hell of a trick. So.

MARGE: So. You understand, then, why I came here, what it is I'm doing here? I repeat—nothing is being determined by just one visit and—

ISAAC: *(Suddenly furious):* They send a woman into my house to see if I'm a whacko, and nothing is being determined here? The—the—the paperwork that has come flying into this apartment from all the—

MARGE: Please, Mr. Geldhart, you have to—

ISAAC: Why the hell don't you just tell me exactly what I have to do?

MARTIN *(In the doorway):* Dad.

ISAAC: Oh, for God's sake, Martin, they sent over here a— look at this woman.

MARGE *(To Martin):* It's okay. Why don't you just leave us for a bit, see how it goes?

ISAAC: Maybe both of you should please just leave me alone. Do you think anyone wants to be seen like this? I mean, it's so fucking vulgar . . .

MARGE *(To Martin):* It's all right.

(Martin looks at Isaac, exits.)

We usually do this at the office. It took a bending of the rules to even get the Department to think about letting someone come to the house.

ISAAC: I see. Well.

MARGE: Your son, Aaron, he wanted it not to be a nightmare for you.

ISAAC: How thoughtful, such a thoughtful boy, always was.

MARGE: Our offices aren't so great. He saw that. He was very protective, and he's quite persuasive. So. Here I am.

ISAAC: Yes, you can imagine how grateful I am that I don't have to go to the Cloisters to see a shrink.

MARGE: Actually, we're not in the Cloisters. We're just around the corner, so to speak, across from Bellevue. *(Beat)* Your son said you might be a little cranky.

ISAAC: A little cranky? Fuck him. That's Aaron's brilliant analysis of my situation, "a little bit cranky"?

MARGE: No, that was Martin. Aaron wasn't so mild.

ISAAC: Aaron. Do you know when last I saw him? Three and a half years ago! Three and a half years. Years!

MARGE: Do you know why I'm here, though? Aside from—

ISAAC *(Cuts her off, savage):* I don't give a shit. Did you hear what I said? Three and a half years, and every day I don't see him is a victory. And as for this one, a couple of times a year and only because he's weaker than the other two, and believe me, I'm not *that* hard. "A little cranky." Fuck them! Tell me something, Miss Hackett. You got any children?

MARGE: Yes, I have children, yeah. I do have children, and—

ISAAC: And do your children think *you're* crazy?

MARGE: Yes.

ISAAC: Do they really? Well then, Bob's your aunt, as the Brits like to say. So, how are things at Sotheby's?

MARGE: Sotheby?

ISAAC: What do you think of the collection?

MARGE: Pardon me? What are you talking about?

ISAAC *(Pointing to some framed letters on the wall):* The illustrated letters. Believe me, I've seen you eyeing 'em. You'll see, just like I said on the phone, the collection—I have one piece that's exquisitely ironic.

MARGE: I'm not from Sotheby. I'm from Social Services.

ISAAC *(Letting that one go):* I have here something that's not up on the walls. . . . There was a filing system when—I used to have Miss Barzakian rummaging around in here doing alphabetical orders and such. The perfect job for a person who was never married. She had an Eastern European's passion for chaos. *(Takes a moment)* Of course, what she is now is dead, of course. You know? And we had a link, let me tell you.

MARGE: What was that? *(Beat)* Mr. Geldhart?

ISAAC: We were both refugees. New York, for some of us, for many, who got out of "that kind of Europe"—how do you explain such a link? We didn't come as husks. We came with some decent socks and some hand-made shoes. Our Europe. *(He stops, looks at her)* But forgive me. You are not interested in this.

MARGE: No, it's interesting.

ISAAC *(Overriding her with a small, sad smile):* No, of course you're not. You came to look at the collection. Forgive me. My mind wanders, so they tell me.

MARGE: Are you toying with me, Mr. Geldhart?

ISAAC: I'm not toying with anyone, Miss Hackett, not at all.

MARGE: Do you mind if I smoke?

ISAAC: Nobody smokes anymore.

MARGE: Well, I do.

ISAAC: Yeah, me too. I'll join you. Must be nuts.

MARGE: At the hospital, they don't permit it. Which seems a kind of one-upsmanship to me. Frankly, you know. Bush the smokers. Lord over 'em. Give it to 'em. And there are all these signs on the wall. Well, it's a hospital, so you can't complain. But they give you these looks. That's even if you step outside. They have this little quadrangle, and they won't even put a *bench* there.

ISAAC *(Lights her cigarette):* Well, that's very interesting, Miss Hackett.

MARGE: And they give you these little breaks. It's all highly regulated. But the very worst of it is, the worst is—there are these women. These insufferable women in white nurses outfits—not even real R.N.s—just volunteers who come in on the Long Island Railroad from *Merrick.*

And they create these little *dramas*. My smoking. That constitutes a drama, so I guess life's lost its luster for them, huh? You should see 'em. They have their own refrigerator, and they put labels on cans of Tab. "Do not touch—Molly's Tab." "Debbie's Tuna." And you're forced into the position of acquiescing to them.

ISAAC: Excuse me, I'm sorry, but, do I make you nervous or something?

MARGE: I can admit that, yes. Why?

ISAAC: Yeah, I know your type. Divorced. New York State College at New Paltz. Tried to be "with it."

MARGE: If it makes you comfortable to create a little scenario for me, fine. Understand that your son Aaron has suggested competency proceedings be—

ISAAC: Please!

MARGE: Because you have demonstrated a credible inability to manage your own affairs.

ISAAC: And what makes you think you could do such a job? Do you have a formal means of determining levels of responsibility? Rational adult behavior? What? Does the Mayor and Cardinal what's-his-name get together? What? The Skinner people, the Sullivan people? Dewey Decimal? At least in the *library* world . . . *(Isaac halts)* No. I can't take this seriously. No.

MARGE: No. Well, neither does your son Martin.

ISAAC: Ah, the Neville Chamberlain of sons.

MARGE: Well, the fact is, we were called upon. It is to be taken seriously.

ISAAC: Did the woman give you a coffee?

MARGE: And you agreed. You said, "Yes." An evaluation was acceptable to you, if it would result in your being left alone. Nobody wants to come into somebody's life and—

ISAAC: You are speaking to me as if I were someone to whom logic was a worthwhile approach. If I am ga-ga, logic means nothing, right?

MARGE: Well, I'm new. Maybe with a little experience, I'll begin treating people badly. Look, I really, all I have to do is ask you some questions. *(She stares at Isaac)* We can get it over with. And—it's not as if what I say can determine your fate. If that's what you're afraid of . . .

ISAAC: What a relief. Okay, shoot.

MARGE: What country, state, city are we in right now?

ISAAC: Are you kidding me? What kind of question is that?

MARGE: It's a perfectly reasonable question.

ISAAC: Next.

MARGE: What month is it?

ISAAC: July, can't you tell?

MARGE: Mr. Geldhart, look—

ISAAC: Okay. There is a book company. It has my name on it. And some forty percent of it still belongs to me. Some Japanese own the rest, along with Aaron, who has helped them grind it down into kind of bankrupt dust. *(Beat)* Now, I am trying to put together a package. I still know a little money in this town and at the same time, my son, also wants to eighty-six the nips, and he thought if he could get me out of the picture, he could use my forty as leverage. This is what we've got here.

MARGE: You're saying your son is doing all this just to get your stock?

ISAAC: So—you are a dupe, sweetie. Now, I've got coffee cake, linzer torte and sacher torte. You want some?

(Nobody says anything for a moment.)

MARGE: Aaron tells me you spent forty-three thousand dollars on hand-cut suits. What made you think you needed them?

ISAAC: I thought it was going to be a busy year.

MARGE: He says you hardly ever leave this apartment. Is that true?

ISAAC: It was *not* a busy year.

MARGE: And that you've cast off all your friends, you've disengaged.

ISAAC: What? I need to have friends?

MARGE: And the credit card bills?

ISAAC: Staggering! Guilty.

MARGE: You're living on—I mean—I don't understand. What

did you think would happen to you when it was all gone?

ISAAC *(With exaggerated good cheer):* Who cares?

MARGE: You were diagnosed last year as chronically depressed. You've been on Elavil three times a day.

ISAAC: I stopped taking it. I couldn't read. That I could not accept. *(Suddenly bright)* Enough of this. Let me show you the collection. You said on the phone that you are a fan of Herzen? Well, I have the first English edition of *Childhood, Youth & Exile*. London. 1921. *(He hands her the Herzen)* How many can there be of that? A private printing of *Pilgrim's Progress*, 1898. All this shelf, private press stuff—Coleridge was here, sold it to Bertie Rota in London. Wordsworth here. *(He picks up a catalogue)* See? The Geldhart Collection. Look at the prices. That's what you get in London where there's still a market, but here. . . . Jack London, and Conrad here. And of course, I still got the illustrated letters. I only sold a couple, to make the Visa people happy. They were getting shrill.

(He sits next to her on the sofa, with the illustrated letters file on the coffee table.)

MARGE: And this is what you love? Books.

ISAAC: Yes. Funny.

MARGE: What? What is it? Did I say something? I—

(She smiles. He is amused.)

ISAAC: No, you had this tone. This marvelous tone. This anti-intellectual tone one comes across. So. You hate books.

MARGE: Not at all.

ISAAC: *(Opening the folder):* There was a time when people used to revel in words. In stories. A kind of perfection, in the air about you, at all times. And people, of course, they used to write. To each other. And how marvelous to accompany the letter with a drawing. A gesture of love—*(Pause)* Thackeray. Look at it. He bombarded friends with letters. Look at the sketches. He used to illustrate his own novels!

MARGE: It's lovely.

ISAAC: Max Beerbohm. Look at this. George Grosz. Here is, from Max Beckmann, a little note, a sketch. They chased him out, he ended up dead in the States. A teacher.

MARGE: Oh!

ISAAC: Osip Mandelstam to his wife. Isaac Babel to his. Orwell from Spain. You begin to see such a blood-thirsty century . . . but aren't they all? Maybe. Maybe, I don't know. *(He looks at her sharply)* Mind you—it's understood from the get-go, you take the entire collection. I can't bear to think of its being split up, divvied up all over town—it's to be sold as a piece or nothing, got it?

MARGE *(After a moment):* It's a lovely collection.

ISAAC: You like it?

MARGE: Very much.

ISAAC *(Clear and quiet and bitter):* Me, too.

MARGE: I'm sorry.

ISAAC: What?

MARGE: Listen, Mr. Geldhart. I'm going to have someone else do this.

ISAAC: What?

MARGE: I'm sorry. Someone will call from my office. I'm not the one to do this. I just hate this. I can't do it.

ISAAC: What? Please, what did I say? Look at the rest of the work, would you?

MARGE *(Rushing to leave):* I'm not from Sotheby, and I shouldn't be here. Goodbye, Mr. Geldhart.

ISAAC I have a letter from Adolph Hitler . . .

MARGE: Mr. Geldhart—

ISAAC: A postcard actually on which he painted a little water-color of a burnt-out church. Bought his art supplies from a Jew. Who thought he had talent. And gave him, just gave him his materials. I mean, I think about that, and what came after. . . . It's the most crucial part of my collection. *(Isaac shows the card to Marge)* He was not without a certain basic, rudimentary talent, was he not? You would certainly hope that he had been utterly devoid of talent. I mean, it would at least shed some tiny glimmer of light on the subsequent years, on all that came after. But no—it's no slur of muddy-non-color, this. There is something here, yes?

MARGE: I suppose.

ISAAC: It's never actually been appraised, which is why I called your firm. So—

MARGE: You don't really think I'm from an auction house, do you, Mr. Geldhart?

ISAAC *(After a moment):* I have problems.

MARGE: Yes.

ISAAC: Oh, I know I'm getting it wrong a lot of the time. I used to think it was the fog from the pills they gave me, but when I stopped taking the pills . . . the fog would not lift. But to simply stand about, helpless. That is not acceptable to me. I am not used to it. *(Beat)* I find my dream life so much more interesting, given my current waking one. *(Beat)* It's getting dark. So early. Every year a little earlier. Have you ever been out into this park?

MARGE: A few times. When my husband was alive.

ISAAC: Oh. I see. Oh. *(Beat)* Sorry.

MARGE: We had friends who lived across the park. They used to promenade us there, yeah. Fine, it's a nice park, but, the idea of a key bugs me. It's just a *park*, for God's sake.

ISAAC: Capitalism at its worst?

MARGE: Just small-minded. I wasn't looking at the politics of the thing.

ISAAC: I've never liked this park. You need a key to get in it. And there's never anyone there.

MARGE: I was here once before.

ISAAC: What was that? What did you say?

MARGE: 1974. During the crisis. The city crisis, when New York was broke, I was here, in this apartment.

ISAAC: You were in my house before? In this apartment?

MARGE: At work, there are these gruesome meetings, at which they assign all the cases. And I recognized your name.

ISAAC: So we *have* met before?

MARGE: You must have had a lot going on in those days. Yes.

And I recognized your name from the caseload, and I didn't say anything. This room is the same. It's not as clean, it's not what it was, but the same.

ISAAC: Forgive me, but I'm lost, I knew I recognized you, but I can't place it, and anyhow, most often, when I think I know someone, I'm wrong. You were here before?

MARGE: There was a reading. Some essayist you published, it was a fundraiser for the library. Because the books were literally rotting, and nobody worked there, and there—

ISAAC: They didn't have a single copy of Joyce's *Exiles*. I went in and exploded.

MARGE: So it *was* a fundraiser.

ISAAC: It was horrible.

MARGE: My husband liked those kinds of things. Mainly for the food. I remember one thing in particular. You didn't have rumaki, which was standard fare for those things, and for that little bit, I was grateful.

(Isaac pours a drink, offers it to Marge. She refuses.)

ISAAC: It *was* a reading. Clayton Broomer, prick of a guy from the *New Yorker*—wrote about architecture. I couldn't stand him, but my wife made me publish his books. He shrilled at everyone in 'em, about how the city got so ugly. Boy, did I hate those things.

MARGE: Me too.

ISAAC: So. Different time, this, eh? Different time.

MARGE *(Tentative):* And we talked.

ISAAC: We talked?

MARGE: We stood in the kitchen. And you were intensely annoyed with your wife.

ISAAC: She had a touch of the flag-waver about her.

MARGE *(Remembering):* We stood in your kitchen, you and I, drinking vodka and smoking. I remember hearing my husband laughing and making some sort of deal in this room. We'd just watched him rip off a whole plate of gravlax from the waitress, and devour it. You were very insulting. You said he had a voice like something from an animal act on Public Television. I might have been hurt but we were enjoying the vodka . . .

ISAAC: Your husband. Tell me, who is this? You sound . . . ?

MARGE: Bitter? Yeah, well . . . *(Pause)* My husband was Adrian Harrold.

ISAAC *(Nods, getting it):* Oh, I see. Jesus Christ. And now ‑you work for social services, shlepping around town with a little briefcase? Adrian Harrold. I remember your husband. The Manhattan borough president. And in the end, made off with a couple of million, right?

MARGE: The last editorial in the *Times* said, "Drinking from the public trough like a maddened pig . . ."

ISAAC: Please, I really, this is not. I did not . . .

MARGE: Do you know how they found him? My husband? On the road to Montauk. Actually, at the end of the road. God knows what he was doing. In February out there, by the lighthouse. He had a Biedermeier table in the back of his Lincoln. His wrists and ankles slashed and a bottle of pills on the floor. And then, for weeks afterwards, the funny part, these women would show up with outrageous claims. *(Beat)* Good for a laugh, at least.

ISAAC: I'm sorry. I am.

MARGE: My husband lied from morning 'til night, and they knew everything. The mayor. All of them. The only one, really, who knew nothing was, in fact, me.

ISAAC: So, your husband, he left you, what? Nothing?

MARGE: No. He left nothing. I mean, he had his hands in the till. And to me, this is funny—he never shared. It was all for him. *(She looks at him)* I expected to find a drooler. I thought I'd come over here and find a drooler who had had it easy in the old days.

ISAAC: No, unfortunately, I'm not a drooler. So, you came not for an "evaluation," you came 'cause you were curious.

MARGE: Yes.

ISAAC: You came to gloat. You came to see a "drooler."

MARGE *(Ashamed, perhaps):* Maybe.

ISAAC: But this is pathetic. It's like nostalgia for a car wreck. So, terrific, you're just another hustler with an agenda.

MARGE: You could say that.

ISAAC: So, what it is is you get a kick out of seeing someone from the old days? And maybe even taking him down? That's a lot of power for the wife of a prick with sticky fingers.

MARGE: Yes.

ISAAC: Well, that's New York. I mean, that's the ultimate. Wonderful. Let me tell you. I came from the worst place. People turning one another in for a hustle, for a piece of ass, for a piece of black bread, whatever. You get it, sweetie? I mean, if they thought you were a Jew, or not. *Or not.* If they were just pissed off at you 'cause you slighted them. But, this city wins on points. You got me? This city wins on points. Because you had a hard-on to see a crony of your crooked husband? Because you were a little lonely, a little weepy for the old days? You come here, raising the lefty flag—you self-righteous, social-worker-tootsie. Tell me, are you going to put in your report to Social Services that you came here for a vodka and a flirt fifteen fucking years ago? You're going to tell them that at Social Services? Hey, let me tell you something, *that* was my wife who did the fundraisers. She dragged every downtrodden threadbare cause into this house, from the Panthers on down. And now *I* should pay 'cause *you're* bitter? *(Pause)* I should pay. Please go home and tell them, go home to your little Smith-Corona, go type up, "He's got delusions of persecution, and he's probably gonna end up like Schwartz, dead."

MARGE: Who? End up like . . . ?

ISAAC: Delmore Schwartz. He said, "Even paranoids have enemies." He used to come here for dinner before he died in the hallway of his hotel. So *arbeit* does indeed *macht frei*, huh?

MARGE: I made a horrible mistake.

ISAAC: What in the world could you possibly think I had to do with your husband? It seems positively lunatic to me. Revenge! My God! You came for revenge!

MARGE: What about you? You don't know anything about revenge?

ISAAC: What are you talking about? What do you mean?

MARGE: Your children! "Every day I don't see him is a victory!" "The Neville Chamberlain of sons!" "Fuck them." You could tell me a whole hell of a lot about revenge, Mr. Geldhart.

ISAAC: Revenge I know.

MARGE: Seems to me revenge is the only thing keeping you alive. I don't walk around Manhattan with a grudge. I don't walk around this city thinking of revenge. It just wells up.

ISAAC: That I understand.

MARGE: But I get out of bed, as bad as it gets. I'm not saying I don't have days where I don't get out of bed. I think I spent most of '88 staring up at my ceiling. But I try. I put one foot in front of the other and—most of the time I don't even know why. I just do it. I just do it. Well, I've got to go.

ISAAC: Miss Hackett, may I ask you to have dinner with me?

MARGE: What are you talking about? You want to have dinner? You kicked me out a minute ago, or don't you remember?

ISAAC: I am a forgiving man.

MARGE: What, you want to sit somewhere? You want to go somewhere and sit at a table?

ISAAC: I think it would be very nice, very good, were we to have dinner.

MARGE: No. That would be crossing a line.

ISAAC: Why? They wouldn't know.

MARGE: I'd get canned. No, worse. I'd have a "letter" put in my personal file.

ISAAC: They don't follow you around. They wouldn't know. What's the big deal? I still have my Diner's Club Card that hasn't been shredded. Gramercy Park has become decent, restaurant-wise. Food is better now than when we were young. No more sauerbraten and schnitzel. You see, there was a time, emigration let some Italians in in the Seventies—they brought with them significant secrets.

MARGE: I don't think so.

ISAAC: It seems to me that all professionalism has already been blown.

MARGE: Nevertheless. We just can't have dinner. I can't start doing this sort of thing, I just can't.

ISAAC: Late in the game for romance?

MARGE: Romance is not even a consideration.

ISAAC: Out of your vocabulary? Well, too bad. Maybe you've had all the human traffic a person can bear.

MARGE: Maybe I have. I look at you and it doesn't look so great for you either.

ISAAC: Tell me, then, what chance do you think you have in this world? I am curious?

MARGE: What do you mean, "chance"?

ISAAC: Yes. "Chance." Exactly. What're you going to do? Wait for a better deal?

MARGE: I'm not waiting for anything. In the last five years I put myself through school and got this job, which admittedly is not what I imagined, but still. What have you *done*, lately? I had to drive out to Long Island with a suit for my husband, because he was wearing jogging pants and a Drexel Burnham tee shirt when they found him. *(Pause)* Chance? Fuck you. Chance? Man, I hope I don't look fragile or give the impression that I'm on some sort of widow's walk. I have a son who knows his father ripped off everything in this city that wasn't nailed down! I watched my husband on news at five, *weeping*. Chance? What chance do I have? Because I won't have dinner with you? *(Beat)* Do you know how much I hate having dinner by myself night after night? Well, I'd rather do that, let me assure you, than have dinner with you and compare bad-break notes.

ISAAC: Why? Afraid you're going to see yourself in me? Is that it?

MARGE: We are nothing alike. Whatever has happened to you, you've done to yourself. You had everything and you threw it away.

ISAAC: I threw nothing away.

MARGE: Then this is how you thought your life would go?

ISAAC: You can't even imagine. You have no idea. This is not how I saw my life going. But surprised I am not, Miss Hackett. I did this to myself. You don't see any other surviviors in your files, do you? You don't see any brothers and sisters? Betrayal? I never even smelt it coming until the fucking *maid* turned us in. The *maid.* She was like my mother, and let me tell you—I don't have self-pity! You don't see a tattoo on my wrist, do you? But they got my grandparents, they got my mother and father, and they got. . . . I came here to make a family and they trashed it., they got it.

MARGE: I am sorry. But really, I am going to leave.

ISAAC: Listen to me. You came here with an agenda, but now at least listen to what was taken away from me. *(Pause)* I loved my children. I sure don't love them now. You walk into this house . . . *(He points to a table)* Aaron cut his head on the tip of that table and I carried him to NYU Hospital when he was two. *(Beat)* Sarah got laid for the first time in this house, and I thought I was quite literally going to die. *(Beat)* My wife found this sofa in Kingston and we had it carted down and we sat on it, and it was the most perfect . . . my wife . . . my wife . . . my wife. *(Beat)* My Martin. He comes in here from Lacrosse when he was sixteen, sneezing, and the next thing, he was, just like that—no blood count at all. *(Beat)* So now I sleep in the living room, because the bedrooms are too much to bear. *(Beat)* I am so stupid, Miss Hackett, I thought that if I published Hazlitt and Svevo, I'd be spared. The silence, Miss Hackett. The silence. Pointless.

MARGE *(Thinks before speaking):* I could never bear to play on my husband's connections. There were people who actually liked him, held a degree of sympathy for him. Because, mainly, he kept quiet. He had a thief's honor. I am owed favors. Specifically. I suppose, I am actually owed *one* favor. The way these things work. Because there are people in this town who actually think my husband *told* me things. Which is rich. *(Beat)* But. I can make a call. I can call a judge. And they'll just drop it. Like that. And believe me, there'd be nothing your son can do.

ISAAC: Wouldn't that make you just like your husband?

MARGE: No—that's too damn tough, that's just too hard. We're just flesh and blood here. That's all we are. *(Beat)* I'm offering you a good hand. What are you gonna do? Wait for a "better deal"? There are so few breaks.

ISAAC *(After a moment):* There are, that's true. *(Beat)* Perhaps you're right. *(Tired)* I *would* like a break.

MARGE: Then it'll be over.

ISAAC: Over? That would be lovely, if it were over. *(He picks up the postcard)* Look at this thing. The man fancied himself a serious artist. Lugging his little brushes about Vienna, God knows. Scraggly hair, greasy. You pick this up. What was the day like when he painted it? What was that sky like? *(Lost for an instant, soft)* All the things to come. So much to come.

MARGE: It's just a lousy postcard. My husband had post-it notes all over the place, and I didn't save them.

ISAAC *(Looking at her with a great, sudden affection):* Goddamn it, it's a pity I could not persuade you to dine with me. I can be amusing. Especially when I take the anti-depressants they prescribe. Then I am at my best. Restaurants are so hard to bear alone.

MARGE: You do not have to eat alone.

(She looks at him for a moment. And turns to exit.)

ISAAC: Miss Hackett? Thank you. Maybe, when the time is more appropriate, when the weather is kinder, we *could* have dinner.

MARGE: That . . . would be nice, Isaac. Good night.

(She exits. Isaac picks up postcard, and then sets it alight. Placing it in an ashtray, he sits looking at it. Snow streams down. The card burns. After a moment, Martin enters.)

MARTIN: She left.

ISAAC: She left. Yes. She's gone, she went.

MARTIN: What is that? What are you doing?

ISAAC: Nothing.

(Beat.)

MARTIN: How was it?

ISAAC: Well, you can relax for a while. You won't have to write my checks and listen to complaints of the cook and make sure that my underwear is changed, for a little while yet.

MARTIN: Of course not. I know that.

ISAAC: So you can relax, you're free.

MARTIN: Well I wouldn't mind. I'd do it.

ISAAC: You would. Yes, you would. Why wouldn't you mind, Martin? I don't understand . . . why you wouldn't mind after this . . . ?

MARTIN: Because I am not, unfortunately, as strong as you.

ISAAC: What does that mean? Martin? Please? What?

MARTIN: I don't know. I don't have it in me to do this thing. This thing that you do: resolving to write people off, to write it all off. I don't. And believe me, I've tried.

ISAAC: And now what? You're going back upstate?

MARTIN: There's a train in forty minutes, yeah. But they're all screwed up. *(He puts on his coat)* So it's good that it worked out with the. . . . Look, you call if you want anything. I'll be up there tonight.

ISAAC: Maybe I'll walk outside with you a bit. It's so lovely with the snow. Do you want to walk through the park?

MARTIN: Sure.

ISAAC: I need to find the key to the park. Let me find the key.

MARTIN: Wait. I've still got mine.

(Martin puts on his coat, hands Isaac his. They walk out to the hall. Martin turns off the light.)

The
End of the
Day

To my friend and agent, George Lane

Playwrights Horizons, Inc., New York City, produced *The End of the Day* Off Broadway in 1992.

The End of the Day was given a workshop production by The Seattle Repertory Theatre in 1990.

Characters

Note: The doubling of roles is a deliberate and important part of the play.

Time

1986, then 1992

Place

Act One

Act Two

SCENE ONE
The Massey-Kitterson home, London

SCENE TWO
The verandah overlooking Belgrave Square

SCENE THREE
San Cristobal Clinic, San Pedro

SCENE FOUR
The same

SCENE FIVE
The same

SCENE SIX
Los Angeles Museum of Art

The
End of the
Day

ACT ONE

Scene One

Prologue. 1986. Malibu Canyon. Offstage, a party. The sounds of the crowd mingle with the brassy roar of a Sixties bossa nova. Graydon Massey, an aristocratic Englishman, is dressing at a leisurely pace. He first wipes off an excess of shaving cream from his face—revealing a handsomeness that comes from yachting, breeding and intelligence. He has a boredom about him even when activated; a skepticism in his expression. On the bed is a linen suit, the color of a summer field of wheat, a white shirt and an impeccable tie of burnt orange. A drink—a Margarita—sits on the table beside a telephone and a cigar. When dressing, Massey often takes a moment for a drag or a swallow.

The view—precisely that of a Southern California canyon at dusk: sun-dappled hills of brush and scrub; houses on stilts that reach upwards, dangling delicately over precipices of cactus and weed and palm. Massey talks to himself as he dresses.

MASSEY: I pledge allegiance to the flag . . . *(He pauses, perplexed, trying to get it right)* . . . to the flag, uh-huh, for which it stands, one nation, and republic . . . under

God . . . invisible . . . inadvisable . . . invisible, some-
thing-something-something and lah-lah-lah. Under
God. Yes. There we are. Liberty and uh . . . *honor* for
all.

HILTON *(Offstage):*   HELEN *(Offstage):*
Graydon. Graydon.   Graydon. Graydon!

*(Massey looks in the mirror, goes on, a narcissist
all the way, practicing his speech, occasionally
referring to a sheet of paper.)*

MASSEY: I want to thank, I really can't escape the inevitability of thanking my family, my American family; my
wife Helen, my father-in-law Hilton Lasker—for . . .
(He thinks) . . . Uh, maintaining, keeping me—sup-
porting me—in such style while I worked on becoming a citizen, and a licensed psychiatrist in America.
The . . . hub . . . of, uh, medicine and . . . uh,
thought—er—medical philosophy of the world. The
fact is, until landing up in Malibu here, I did not feel
quite alive, so I think, *ich bin un Malibuan.* In my
heart. *(He thinks again, nods to himself, liking it)*
From the moment I stepped off of the aeroplane and
onto the tarmac on that sweltering day in February
some six years ago, I have felt entirely at home—and
occasionally while driving, I ask myself: what does it
mean to be an American? It means . . . taking on . . . a
grave responsibility . . . *(He thinks for a moment,
shrugs, goes on)* Which one often is tempted to avoid.
. . . In my America, when Hilton, my dear father-in-
law, takes me to a Dodger game, I experience a unity
that Englishness precludes—but here—Tommy
Lasorda and Frenesco Venezuela . . . Pat Riley, these
people and, I—Quincy Jones, Wolfgang Puck—all
brothers.

HILTON *(Offstage):*   HELEN *(Offstage):*
Graydon. Graydon.   Hon, everyone's waiting.

MASSEY: Just a moment darling. . . . Because we have shared
a dream of America—I look at my family here today,
and I believe many of you have parents and grandparents who—who came over in steerage from er—

Cracow and Minsk to hustle scraps in America—and now here one finds oneself in 1986—rested, healthy, grateful, at peace—an American. *(He takes a moment, reads back, smiling)* At my citizenship hearing the other day, we were discussing what it is that makes this country great, and I brought this notion of an "example," as it were, as sort of—"My favorite American," so to speak, which is—as we've talked about in the family—we know—Richard Nixon, because he exemplifies what is America—a greatness in that—one of your great writers, F. Roy Fitzgerald said "There are no second acts in American life," and Richard Nixon gives evidence to that lie—because he really emerged as the winner—from five o'clock shadowy-felon to elder statesman in a decade. *(Beat)* The point is, in America, you can reinvent yourself. You can become yourself and nowhere else in the world is this thing possible— what I said to the immigration officers as they were deciding was—"In America, there is nothing to stop one from going back for seconds." In America—you can go back for seconds. . . . Right. *(Beat. Massey adjusts his tie)* Right.

Scene Two

Massey looks at the view, sighs, and moves to walk out into the party—as he does so, the world changes around him; the world we are now in is the direct antithesis of the Malibu canyon house. Six years have passed—we are in Massey's office at the San Cristobal Clinic in San Pedro near the L.A. harbor. It is dreary, dark; the glass on the door is green, sends in a green light from outside; and there is a sense of a sort of vast Dantesque hell of patients just outside, moaning. The wall is lined with public health posters on a variety of topics: all with graphic illustrations, all in Spanish. Massey sits at his desk, on the phone, bored.

MASSEY: Now look, Father Zapollian or Zapotec or whomever the hell you are—yo no want-o fight-o con you-o on el telephone-o. In my considerable experience, trusting and believing in junkies is a bit of a rum bet and I don't care if he's a third generation altar boy up for beatification, he sure as fuck doesn't bother bleaching his needles. *(Beat. Massey smiles, enjoying this)* Yes, no, and yes, while it's true that I haven't much experience in the barrio, and nor do I particularly care to, and furthermore, *furthermore,* get with it pal. This is 1992, so please don't think that lording over me with your church prole superiority is going to have me all humble and mumbling all over the place. Look, Father Zamoulian, what I'm trying to tell you is, I don't mind pissing you off—I'm willing to slip you, from the hospital, bloody great cartons full of clean needles and you could, instead of standing about performing last rites on these people, perhaps keep a few about this mortal coil for a bit, and—and—and if that makes you happy, how's about I send along a couple hundred boxes of rubbers, French letters, ribbed ticklers—condoms— and, instead of lounging about drinking the blood of Christ all fucking day, hand them out too, instead of trusting your pathetic, rickets-ridden, louse-infested, illiterate flock to the odds which don't look all that swell for junkies! *(He slams down the phone with great relish, and lights a smoke before once again picking up the phone)* Nurse—Cantillion or whatever you're called, where do you people keep the hypodermics, and all that? Well, it's only my first week and— yes, I'm sorry, I know I was rude to the priest, but would you mind, my sweet, not listening in on my calls in the future? I know I'm new and you haven't gotten used to me and perhaps the previous resident didn't mind spying, I do. *(Beat. He grins)* Would you be so kind as to now send in the next patient, uh . . . Toffler, yes. Hilly Lasker's here? Good God in heaven, tell him I'm not in.

(He hangs up the phone. Hilton Lasker enters.

*Massey's father-in-law. A big, overly handsome
man in a cheapo James Coburn sort of way and
far too rich—an AFL-CIO type gone bad, with
millions of bucks the end result. He plainly
adores Massey utterly.)*

HILTON: Man, am I proud of you kid, this is a major step for
you, working here. You get to fight your own selfish-
ness. Can't be a snob here.

MASSEY: Not for a second, hello. Hilly. Yes, I was expecting
you'd show up just about now. How's Helen?

HILTON: Best thing ever happened to her, you walking out.

MASSEY: Not exactly sure how I should take that, old man.

HILTON: The whole ninety yards. She's not doing so great,
but that's neither here nor there. I was down at the
harbor, I've got eleven tons of kiwi fruit sitting on the
dock from Christchurch, New Zealand and a restaurant
workers' strike, so it's all rotting, anyhow, I stood
there, it smells so sweet, I was sick, I thought, "Why
not come see how you're doin'?" *(Beat)* So. Big change
this, isn't it, from El Camino Drive behind the Beverly
Wilshire, isn't it?

MASSEY: You're telling me, mate. I've seen fifty people in my
three days here, and forty-seven and a half of them are
dying. Different. Yes.

HILTON: Sweetie, all of us are dying. They paying you anything down here?

MASSEY: Thirty-one five. Something like that. Thirty-two,
three maybe.

HILTON: Well I know there must be some people in this bitter world who live on that kind of money, kid—but I
don't know who they are or where they are.

MASSEY: Oh come off it, Hilly. What is it? I know you.
You're here to make trouble for me. Well let me tell
you, pal, I won't have it. You've probably all decided to
have my legs broken.

HILTON: You're my son-in-law, I love you, I'm sick over this
whole thing.

MASSEY: Under no circumstances am I coming back to your
daughter, Hilly, so you can just forget it.

HILTON: Back? Listen, I love you. You came into our lives and I had never seen an item like yourself—one of the major items I ever met. I just want us still to be able to go to Dodger games and the track together.

MASSEY *(Appeasing):* Well you know I'd hate to give that up, but maybe it's—

HILTON *(Cuts him off, slightly nasty):* Yeah, yeah, yeah, fine. But I'm circling my point. There is an issue deeply troubling to me and I respect you too much to let it pass. And it has to do with cleaning of the slates. An item which has become an important one on your agenda.

MASSEY: Well, go on, Hilly, yes, cleaning the slate is . . . *(Pause. He looks suspiciously at Hilton)* What exactly do you mean, precisely?

HILTON *(Low and dark and sly):* I have an accounting for you and if you're serious about this big change and ya want it to be clean, we really have to address it.

MASSEY: A bloody *what?* An accounting?

HILTON: I have a fiduciary responsibility to my daughter, Graydon? Can you please understand that? This is mortifying to me!

MASSEY: You love it! Look at you, you're practically Jimmy bloody Hoffa standing here extorting money from me! Shame on you, you pathetic bloody hoodlum!

HILTON: I'm a restaurant supplies dealer and produce wholesaler! I'm no big shot, Gray! I bleed at night! I lie there bleeding! I have skyrocketing insurance and trucks that break down and a huckster is what I am, a huckster. I look for a deal on tomatoes. You've always had me wrong! It's not *Guys and Dolls* and that guy de Tocqueville's big fucked-up America you practically shoved down my throat; it's a guy—who has to make a buck—and think about his kids! *(Beat)* So you walked—hey, that's cool, man, terrific. I wish, I only wish I could too. But the fact is—I have an accounting.

(Pause.)

MASSEY: And exactly how much would that be, precisely, Hilton?

HILTON: Seven hundred and thirty-six thousand dollars, for- get the cents. I'm no vulgarian.

MASSEY *(Laughs):* Hilly, oh, Hilly, how marvelous. What a card, what a maroon.

HILTON: A—we bankrolled your American internship, 2— we bankrolled your practice when you thought you wanted to be a shrink, C—when you didn't want to be a shrink and you wanted to be an oncologist, we paid for you to go back to med school, 5—we paid the rent on the Malibu Canyon house, 9—a Peugeot and repairs, E—a thirty-six foot ketch and mooring at Marina Del Rey, L—when you wanted an ad on cable . . . *(Beat)* The suits, the hats, the trips, the—

MASSEY *(Cutting him off):* I have no money, you shark- toothed capitalist prick! Don't you know how wiped- out that practice left me?

HILTON *(Thuggish, suddenly. Rather animal-like):* You left Helen. *(Beat)* And without consulting me. When it all started piling up for you, who was there for you? See? You've got a lot to learn about being an American, kid. We take care of people, that's what we do. And I was proud, because my own son, Max, is my greatest disap- pointment in a life of disappointments!

MASSEY: I wish you wouldn't do that, Hilly, put Max down to glorify me—Max is profoundly emotionally retarded and you stint him in every aspect.

HILTON: See? See? See? That's the side of you one's always loved—so compassionate. So—hey. What was it with Helen, she's my daughter but you can tell me like we're pals—it was a bedroom thing, wasn't it? Is that it? Couldn't let go?

MASSEY: That allegation is beneath my dignity in terms of actually, er, dignifying with a response; however, you're in the ball park.

HILTON *(Excited):* But if that's all it is, then—

MASSEY: For God's sake you vulgarian!

HILTON *(Screaming):* Why? Why break the dream?

MASSEY: Because I haven't felt a thing in years. Anything. Days without feeling, Hilly. Months, years.

HILTON *(Beat. He calms himself):* I feel, in losing you, that I have utterly failed. You were Helen's only hope—that's why we gave you everything. *(Miserable. Confessional. Pleading)* I can't afford to set her up again . . .

MASSEY *(Howling with laughter):* That is the most ludicrous bit of play-acting I've ever seen!

HILTON *(Suddenly cool, lights a smoke, seems like a twenty-five-year old agent at his iciest):* Maybe it is, Gray, but this has to be addressed, son, there's no way to just walk away here. If you think that's the case, you've underestimated us as schmucks and patsies which we're not.

MASSEY: Hilton. What're you proposing?

HILTON: Your family has great wealth.

(Pause. Massey nods, suddenly tired.)

MASSEY: Oy. Well there we are. The worm turns. *(Gentle, patient as if to a nine-year-old)* Hilton. You know they don't speak to me. My coming to America was grounds for excommunication. It's like Edward and Mrs. Simpson to them. You know that. And you know what the English are like—they don't forgive and embrace like us, they chill, ossify, gather evidence, make a case, a file, use it—forever! Sweetie, I'm terribly sorry, but there's no chance of my getting anything out of them; not since we went over in '82 and Helen made them go to *Annie* on the West End with us. That was it.

HILTON: I don't want it to be easy for you, I just want it done. Three quarters of a mil and change.

(Beat. Massey goes and looks out at the harbor.)

MASSEY: It's odd, you know, having rather loved you all. I was just thinking how much I had loved all of you— more sideshow, really, than family, I must confess. And as a family, you know, rather more than I loved Helen. *(Beat)* My big farting sweating lying corrupt yank family, hustling over the lox on Sunday morning, the football on in the background drowning everything out, how much I loved all that—

HILTON: Then go back to her. And we can forget all this strong-arm crapola that makes me sick to my stomach to do. Gray, Gray, Gray. The big truth is this: You can't just walk away from your life in this life.

(The phone rings—LOUD—jarring both of them. Hilton leans to pick it up, Massey grabs it.)

MASSEY: *My* phone! *(Into phone)* Yes. Yes nurse, I know Mr. Toffler is waiting. I'll be with him in a minute, Nurse Lapis Lazuli. *(He hangs up)* Well well, what could you—how could you make me, er, you know? Pay? . . . Hilton? For God's sake, listen to reason.

HILTON: You know, because you changed nationalities, you think—*(He struggles)* Sometimes I think it's all been too easy for you, and I tell you this 'cause I love you and I always will no matter what you force me to do, I'll always love you, maybe a person like you—who can give up his country—something has to matter. If not family, Graydon, what? Money?

MASSEY: Rather unhappy 'bout the turn our relationship is taking, Hilly, and I think it best to quit while we're ahead lest things be said that later are regretted, eh? Asking me for money? Have you no shame?

IIILTON *(Pained):* Graydon, making a buck is a hard, bitter fuck of a trick, especially in this town. They laugh at you on the street in this town, if they don't like your shoes, they laugh—I walked into Spago's with my blue hush puppies and they spit on me. I'm saying—I've been too many hours in the whorehouse, pal—got it?—too many hours bending over and I may be a fool but one thing is assured—this ball can roll seven ways from Sunday but it stops at me getting fucked by you. Is this clear to you?

MASSEY: What're you saying?

HILTON: Pay, stay, or I'll kill you. One of the above, maybe two. But you're not going to close the cart after the horse is gone.

(Phone rings. Massey picks it up.)

MASSEY *(Into phone):* Massey. I see. *(He hangs up the phone)* Two of my patients—not that I've ever met them—just died. And I have to sign the death certificates. See yourself out, Hilton—you louche.

(Massey exits.)

HILTON: Ah, this fuck òf a life. Cocksucker of a life. *(He picks up the phone)* Honey, get me an outside line here. Relax, sweetheart, it's local.

(Toffler enters.)

TOFFLER: I've been waiting six hours, seven if you count filling in a form and eight if you count the time it took them to take out the body of the guy waiting ahead of me.

HILTON: Maybe you're not eating enough vegetables.

TOFFLER: Excuse me?

HILTON: I'm not the doctor, kid.

TOFFLER *(Laughs):* Oh, Christ.

HILTON: But the doctor's not bad. He'll be back in a sec.

(Hilton exits. Massey enters.)

MASSEY: Mr. Toffler?

TOFFLER: Yeah.

MASSEY: You're white.

TOFFLER: Is that going to be a problem? *(Beat)* You wouldn't happen to be a doctor by any chance, would you?

MASSEY: Come in, sit down, what'd you prefer? I'd actually prefer it if I could just call you Jonathon.

TOFFLER: Actually, I'm scared. Sorry, so call me whichever, it's fine.

MASSEY: It is pretty bloody frightening down here, isn't it?

TOFFLER: Well, believe me, if I could pay, I'd go somewhere else. I don't have any money.

MASSEY: Well, I'm just a doctor, I'm not an administrator, you don't see any bouncers, do you?

TOFFLER: The last doctor made me go through a series of, I don't know, it was, you know, it was like an IRS audit, so . . . I'm not actually sure he was a doctor. He never said he was a doctor.

MASSEY: Your file says you've got no insurance. Believe me, you've come to the right place.

TOFFLER: Why are we talking about money, I'm just curious?

MASSEY: Why not? No, just kidding. So. You've come to the right place.

TOFFLER: You're a Brit.

MASSEY: Is that going to be a problem?

TOFFLER: Not for me, it isn't.

MASSEY: So, you've walked in off the streets, then? And you've got nobody, right?

TOFFLER: No, he's already dead. *(Beat)* You haven't read my file.

MASSEY *(Laughs)*: At this place? I've been here—this is my third day here—you must be patient, takes 'em a week just to lose it, and then, well, you know, you hope for the best, see if it actually gets to your desk . . . *(Beat)* A joke.

TOFFLER *(A slight smile of acknowledgment)*: Hey, look, sure. I've just got all the time in the world, haven't I?

MASSEY *(Looks down at the file, reads, nods)*: None of us has forever, Jonathon.

TOFFLER: This is a hell of a bedside manner you've got here, you must be well-liked.

MASSEY: None of us has forever, but you've got as good a chance as any. Your test came back.

TOFFLER: I don't understand, exactly . . .

MASSEY: Negative. You are quite negative, when it comes to HIV. You didn't know this?

TOFFLER: No I didn't, I had no idea . . . I mean, Christ.

MASSEY: Wait a second, they didn't tell you? I mean, it came back days ago, really. Days. Absolute utter-fucking-days ago.

TOFFLER: I called. Every day, Nurse Carlino said—

MASSEY: She's anti-competent.

TOFFLER: And I just assumed, you know? Fait accomplis, 'cause all I've done for the past year and a half is take care of Howard. And at a certain point, you know, sorry, waking up with this other person's shit on my body from having slept next to him, one's perceptions begin to naturally be informed by . . .

MASSEY: Naturally, no, sure, right, no, exactly. But still. Negative.

TOFFLER: I suppose I should be relieved. But still, I feel pretty awful.

MASSEY: Yes well, your blood count's awful, maybe you're borderline leukemic, and also, you have some swelling in your neck, so, sure, be relieved—with the other, it's cut and dried, but with a bit of lymphoma or leukemia, there are some shades of gray. You're exhausted all the time?

TOFFLER: Who isn't?

MASSEY: *(Smiles, wry):* Good point. You're in decent spirits? No next of kin. . . . No family . . .

TOFFLER: They're not a factor.

MASSEY: Well, let me tell you, we'd best go looking for a tumor, do a biopsy. If we find one, we take it out. No discussion, no waiting. Well. We'll go find someone in radiology down there. Find someone who knows something. See where we are. Let's see, monitor the blood count. Then maybe a marrow transplant or something. Maybe we can get lucky. I can round up a couple of other doctors or something.

TOFFLER *(Deciding that he likes Massey):* And then we all go home, right?

MASSEY *(Smiles, touched):* At the end of the day, yes, we do.

(Toffler rises and looks out at the San Pedro Harbor.)

TOFFLER: You know, you wait for this kind of stuff to happen. *(Beat)* I spent all of last year taking care of a man who I was not—at a certain point—in love with any longer. In fact, right before he got sick, I was right at the cusp of leaving, because I was rather bored out of my skull with him. *(Beat)* Wasting my time, with Howard the bore—the biggest annihilation of time since Ferme split the atom. But, you know, I'm no sociopath, me. Howard the bore gets sick—I stay, and—and you know, it uhm, finally it was just manners that made me stay. Just manners, because—if I had found a way to work it out with myself—I'd have packed up, I'd have been out of there. *(Beat)* When they die, when they go, it's a relief. Because, as scary as the silence is, it's better than watching them thin out in front of you. You keep also, experiencing little moments that remind you of what it was like before he was sick—*(Beat. He laughs)* You're a doctor, you know how strong you have to be to get through this, and how much help you need—I have never made many friends—I'll have no visitors, I'm saying you can't win for losing, because I don't know whether that's better or worse—the guilt of—the embarrassment of bringing friends in to watch you waste—*(Miserable, spent, quiet)* I am, really, finally, I guess, grateful that I'm alone, because if being sick alone is hell then after that, what is there to scare you? Nothing. Nothing.

MASSEY: My job requires me to tell you not to be hasty, not to give up, and probably, fighters—if it's in your nature—end up doing better in this situation.

TOFFLER: There's this line. Heartbreaking sort of line—being sick is going to a foreign country. Flannery O'Connor line.

MASSEY: You might just have a round trip ticket, old boy. *(Pause)* I don't want to be too Zen-passive and eastern about this—we're a county hospital—put yourself in the hands of the nurse outside who looks a bit like Spiro Agnew and let me see if I can get in touch with someone.

TOFFLER: Someone?

MASSEY: Experts, specialists. Try not to go mad with fear and wrath and all, Jonathon, for whatever it's worth.

TOFFLER: What does that mean?

MASSEY: You probably think too much.

TOFFLER *(Exiting, a small laugh):* I'll do what I can.

(Massey sits alone for a moment, getting his bearings. A piece of plaster falls to the floor. The phone buzzes, Massey slaps it, then picks it up.)

MASSEY: Would you mind very much not bothering me every couple of minutes, darling, and bring me a pot of Russian Caravan tea, chop-chop nursie—what? By the way, Nurse Pantiloonie, I'm sorry if we seem to be getting off on the wrong footings here, but really, I think it's best that you being the nurse, adjust to me, rather than I, the doctor, adjusting to you. It's an orthodox little class structure, but where I come from, baby, it's worked just fine for thousands of years. Yes, I know, your name is Mantilini, I shan't get it wrong again. *(He gently puts down the phone)* Cunt.

(Jeremiah Martón enters. Massey's age and of the same patrician class. He wears a Milanese suit of summer cut.)

MARTÓN: Graydon. Good God is it really you?

MASSEY: Good bloody Christ in hell; Jeremiah Martón, is that really you?

MARTÓN: I must tell you; I've never seen anything like this place; it's an absolute maze of the dying. I passed three dead people on my way to you—in their beds, with the IV's still dripping blithely away, saw a nurse taking the temp on a corpse using an anal, orally, chap was dead, but still, dignity's out the window, isn't it? Hello, Graydon, yes, it's me. May I come in please, old chap?

MASSEY: But of course!

MARTÓN: I never thought to see you in such a place.

MASSEY: What the hell are you doing in America?

MARTÓN: Ah, well, we all end up here, sooner or later, don't we? I'm medical advisor on a picture. They're shooting here in San Pedro, though it's meant to be the Congo—though this place passes. I love the way all the palm trees have rats in them here in California. Forgive me, but last I heard you were raking up the bucks in Beverly Hills, you were shrink to the London ex-pat movie colony and their mates.

MASSEY: Well . . .

MARTÓN: Yes, I get it; you do one day a week down here as some sort of gesture towards decency? Nice dodge, eh? Get a write-off, win some points upstairs, cover all the bases, eh. Psychiatry for the out-of-sight poor.

MASSEY: Actually, no, Jeremiah, you see, I'm no longer a shrink. I'm in the oncology game now, trying to make a go of it. I gave up the practice and went back to school, just finished.

MARTÓN *(Momentarily stunned)*: Graydon Massey of Belgrave Square, are you sure it's you?

MASSEY: We studied at London Hospital for Skin Diseases together, old boy.

MARTÓN: Yes, it must be you.

MASSEY: But this is very odd, because last time I saw you, mate, you were a red-toothed commie all rabid for socialized medicine all over the place, hope of the working class and now here you are working on a picture.

MARTÓN: Well, London, like Leningrad, has changed, Gray.

MASSEY: Well then, Jeremiah, so have I. So have we all.

MARTÓN *(A tired, wry sigh)*: Yes. Me? I'm doing an AIDS picture. Totally homophobic, I mean, in the last draft they had mosquitos swarming out of gay bars headed straight for the suburbs. With a voice-over going "Watch the skies, don't take your eyes off the skies!" So, I'm trying to keep the slightly more lurid science fiction aspects under control. So I tell myself I've still got a political context.

MASSEY: Watch the skies?

MARTÓN: Yes, well, my ex-wife tells me I'm just a bent ex-doctor cashing in for the cookie jar. But you! You! You were found all night at the casinos running up and down Mayfair in that little Morgan and your mum had millions. What's all this about, mate?

MASSEY: *(Starts to cry):* I don't know, Jeremiah, I don't know.

MARTÓN: Why Graydon, you're crying. Did I say something beastly? I'm sorry.

MASSEY: No, it's not you, it's ridiculous, it's absurd. *(Beat)* I suddenly missed London for the first time since I've been gone. Lately I've felt so foreign. I voted in their last election. I'm a citizen now. I went into the polling booth and was sucked into two hundred years of history which had nothing to do with me and which I had no interest in—all gerrymandering and carpetbaggers and those bastards I had to vote for—!

MARTÓN: But what you left behind was no better, Gray. The

last one was Stalin in a wig, a cunt. A Medusa; anyone looked at her—straight to stone. The new one's a concierge, a head waiter at a provincial grill, is all. A world of vulgarians.

MASSEY: Yes but she was *our* cunt, he was *our* waiter—they were *our* vulgarians. These people! Ahh, Lord, I'm sorry, I am, I'm simply flooded, hearing your voice. Reminds me of the old days, that particularly English smell of formaldehyde and then off to Soho at three in the morning after rounds for a samosa and a whore. What about our classmates? What happened to them all?

MARTÓN: Stinky Laetner does liposuction behind Fortnum's, Ross DuWitt—abortions for right wing MP's in Pretoria, cleaning up, and Victor Frame—get this— doing chemical warfare research for the Yanks at some joint out near Penzance—this—as NATO packs up its bags, still going on—dies—of an advanced strain of laboratory manufactured botulism—a suicide.

MASSEY: What a horrid lot we were.

MARTÓN: So you've got a hell of a lot to cry about if you ask me. Anything to drink here?

(Massey pulls out a bottle of tequila and a glass from his drawer, picks up the phone.)

MASSEY: Bring me some ice, chop-chop nursie. Are you there? . . . *(Slams the phone down, pours)* You were married?

MARTÓN: She was my beard; typical story, religious parents, a small inheritance I was trying to protect, didn't work, they knew I was playing the men's rooms all along, gave me the money anyway, not much after taxes and all . . . to have to hide like that, shameful, really.

MASSEY: Whole world's gone mad.

MARTÓN: But really lovely tequila, isn't it?

MASSEY *(Wipes his eyes, drinks):* I was brought up to be so terribly strong, Jeremiah, and now nothing I've learnt does me any good whatsoever. They nearly pulled my license and I've no friends or family because I've been a wretched poisonous shit to everybody.

MARTÓN: Seem nice to me, old boy.

MASSEY: Do you think so? I don't suppose you've got a spare million bucks lying round, on the off chance . . .?

MARTÓN: I actually came to ask you the same thing, pal.

MASSEY: Oh I'm flat broke, mate.

MARTÓN: That's rather a pity, a bloke like you with no cash, no point is there?

MASSEY: I don't mind so much, I mean, I was beginning to like the idea of being light.

MARTÓN: Then why'd you just ask for money?

MASSEY: They're rough on you in this country if you don't pay up on your debts. What do you need money for?

MARTÓN: It's quite simple really. We're shooting parts of the picture in Central America. Where precisely I won't mention except to say the transport boat has been fitted by the production carpenters with a fabulous set of false hulls and I thought you might like to make a quick bundle.

MASSEY: I don't like the picture business, really, and as I said I—

MARTÓN: Oh God, no, the picture's a dead loss, no that's not it at all, lad.

MASSEY: Then . . . ?

MARTÓN: Cocaine. Cocaine. Cocaine. Cocaine. Follow?

MASSEY: Pardon?

MARTÓN: Blow.

MASSEY: Jeremiah, are you mad? This is outrageous. You can't possibly be serious.

MARTÓN *(Instantly disgusted):* Ohh, don't. Ohh, *spare me.* Please. I have spent my entire life watching the thieves and ponces get rich. Yes. You know, if you've been brought up with some sort of value system and you stick to it, you're fucked. I watched those hearings on telly. Iran-amuck. They all make off like the thieves of Baghdad—and we're stuck with our plates of greasy fish 'n' chips. *(Beat)* No, no. No, *spare me* "outrageous."

MASSEY: Yes but still, *really.*

MARTÓN: And your own family back home practically swallowing the entire London docks in one sitting? No, no,

no. *Spare me "outrageous".* We live, Graydon, in case
you hadn't noticed, on a very trashy little planet.

MASSEY: But you were going to run for Camden Town
Council.

MARTÓN *(Weeping suddenly):* I'm a wasted man. I've had all
my convictions—political—social—all of it—turned
into so much Stilton cheese for me.

MASSEY: But you mustn't think you can outsmart the
Americans; they have a primitive animal cunning
when it comes to this sort of business, believe me, I
know. There's always a patsy, and it's sure to be you.
Believe me, they've swallowed me, virtually, with a
glass of tap water.

MARTÓN *(Sniffs):* Yes. You do seem diminished. This ghastly
little hospice.

MASSEY: You're making a terrible, wretched mistake,
Jeremiah. Your entire life will be ruined before this
business is over, and what for?

MARTÓN: Money.

MASSEY: *(Violent)* God, how I hate this poisonous country.
What a mistake I made coming here to all the scam
artists and hucksters they've got. They set 'em loose on
you just as you think you've acclimatized—just as
you're getting over the shocking vulgarity of the place,
and started to like it, it turns out they've been planning
all the while to slit your throat and leave you for dead
in an alley!

(The two drink with grim determination.)

MARTÓN: You know, if you were to go in with me on this,
well, you'd beat them at their own game finally.
Nobody comes 'round in Stowe-on-the-Wold offering
a chance at five million beaners, do they? They bloody
well don't. Invite you to the church league cat show if
you're lucky. Wonderful tequila.

MASSEY: From Oaxaca. Should've stayed down there opened
up a nice little Laetrile clinic pulled in all the terminal
cases—the Malcolm Lowry Laetrile Clinic—and then
run like a thief. None of your Beverly Hills types all

afloat in their own Hollywood-Buddhist-checkbook urinary anguish.

MARTÓN: Have a toot of this, practically uncut.

(Takes out a lovely sterling silver pillbox filled with white powder.)

MASSEY *(Rolls a bill. Sniffs. White all over his nose):* I won't go in with you, I'm telling you, it's totally immoral and *thoroughly* passe, I won't be party to such a venture, God how I miss this sort of thing.

MARTÓN *(Takes the bill and does the same):* Well it's a pity to see you wasting away at this ghoulish little morgue—to see a man who had it all reduced to changing bedpans for the nearly dead impoverished Yankee masses.

(There is a further moment with the tequila. Rosamund Brackett enters. A tired, attractive woman, she's seen sixty without flinching.)

BRACKETT: Doctor Massey, may I have a word with you?

MASSEY *(Snaps, from the depths of his booze and coke haze):* Isn't there any fucking privacy in this place? Doesn't anybody know the—the meaning of anybody else's bloody dignity? Eh? How the hell are we supposed to work, Mrs. Brackett, with this kind of impertinence—eh?

BRACKETT: I know this is new to you and a step down.

MASSEY: *(Snaps, savage):* You're damn right, missy.

(Martón giggles like a delighted schoolboy.)

Uhh. This is my distinguished colleague, Doctor Jeremiah, he's visiting the states on behalf of the Queens Medical Trust . . . and er Surgical . . . Command . . . er *Group.* Of Surrey. And is a noted Epidemiological Expert.

MARTÓN: And chiropodist. As well.

MASSEY: He was going to take a look at Mr. Toffler as a courtesy.

BRACKETT: How very lovely.

MARTÓN: Nice to meet ya.

MASSEY: Rosamund Brackett, administrix of our tiny bit o' Calcutta here, on the Pacific.

(There is silence.)

BRACKETT: Could we have a moment alone, please, Doctor Massey? If it's not too much of a burden on your heavy recreational schedule?

MARTÓN: Forgive me! Please, Doctor Massey, I'll just wander the wards and then you can finish your brilliant dissertation on depression and cancer for me over a spot of tea?

MASSEY: Of course dear boy.

(Martón exits. Bracket shakes her head.)

BRACKETT: You boys are so very civilized, aren't you? A real kick in the rump to a broad like me, right? Look. A couple of things: the nurse. Her name is Carlino. Not Manicotti or Borsalino.

MASSEY: I'm dreadful with ethnic names, all a glottal blur . . . sorry.

BRACKETT: Is this it? This is how you get your kicks? Schoolboy meanness? You're not at Eton, doc, you can't get away with teasing your lessers here. As much fun as that may be.

(Pause. Massey acknowledges. A small, sharp shrug and nod.)

MASSEY: Got it.

BRACKETT: And there's Father Zapotec. His Latino Rehab Project may be useless but it gets us federal funding. They see "Latino Blah-Blah Outreach . . ." and we're eligible for a hunk of cash, so don't fuck with him, I need the check. Got it?

MASSEY *(Hugely enjoying her):* Gotcha. Anything else?

BRACKETT: Yeah.

MASSEY: What?

BRACKETT: Do yourself a favor, doc, don't dress so well.

MASSEY: I beg your pardon?

BRACKETT: Hey. I know what you're up to, buddy. Don't "I

beg your pardon" me. You heard. Don't come down here showing off, lording over these people in your arrogant linen suits.

MASSEY: Good Lord.

BRACKETT: It's shitty and small-minded and don't think these people are too dumb to notice. You think you're doing people favors here? Is that it? Hey. Whatever need you had to degrade yourself by coming down here doesn't mean a thing to us. Listen. Leave Beverly Hills behind, pal. And we'll all be better off. Got it?

MASSEY: *(Slow. Relishing her)*: Listen, darling. You stick to administration. Keep out of my way. I'm the only doctor you've got that speaks English and the only one who knows anything about oncology! So let me just tell you to go fuck yourself. I'm not impressed. And furthermore, get me another nurse, would you? Nurse Tintoretto *smells*!

BRACKETT: Oh, a tough customer, huh? Finished?

MASSEY: Not at all. And as for Father Zapotec. Let me remind you that in this country there exists something called separation of Church and State and I'm an employee of the latter and will not bow and scrape to the peasant ignorance of the former. Especially when it's all rolled up into one gruesome little pious lefty spic! Got it?

BRACKETT *(Laughs. Enjoying herself)*: Wow. Let me tell you something, pal. When I fire you, and I *shall* fire you, how I will enjoy it, baby.

MASSEY *(Sighs. Shakes his head)*: I'm sorry, Rosamund. I've had too much coke and too much booze and it's made me all aggressive. Do forgive me. I'm a bit of a Jekyll and Hyde now and then. May I take you to dinner and perhaps a show?

BRACKETT: Out of the question but I'm flattered. Also, Toffler. Medi-Cal won't pay. They sent an investigator. He's got money. His family's got money. He's got 48 hours to pay. He's hiding his dough, we get that sometimes.

MASSEY: No, I don't think he does, actually. Besides, he's going to go out of here in a coffin. Why would he be here if he could help it?

BRACKETT: I ask myself the same thing about you. God knows the reasons people have. Look. He comes from money. I read the report.

MASSEY: Jesus, all anyone talks about is "Money." I'm sick to death of it. It's worse down here than in Beverly Hills!

(Pause.)

BRACKETT: His bed. Must be accounted for. It's not just "A Bed." If the State won't pay, we don't have it to spare.

MASSEY: I'll pay. Sick to death of all of you.

BRACKETT: Doctors paying for patients is strictly forbidden.

MASSEY: Who says?

BRACKETT: It's in the Hippocratic oath, kiddo. You should know that. I need payment within 48 hours or he's out. *(She smiles, appraising him)* Twenty some years ago you could've bought me off with a trip to Palm Springs, a martini by the pool and a roll in the hay. Isn't life funny that way?

MASSEY: What happened?

BRACKETT: Timing, doctor, bad timing.

MARTÓN *(Enters):* Mind you don't slip. There's been a plasma spill in the hall, darling. Wouldn't want to trip down here.

BRACKETT: Thanks, I'll look into that.

(She's gone. Massey sits, spent.)

MARTÓN: You've reconsidered?

MASSEY: Oh please. Go away! Stop bedeviling me!

MARTÓN: Damn you, Massey, don't you see? A man like you—don't throw it all away down here! In this little . . . franchise of hell! For years I've admired you; for my sake, don't deflate like everyone else I've respected and adored! I beg of you!

(He inhales cocaine. Two men with white noses. Helen Lasker-Massey enters; a blowzy, attractive, smart blond. She watches them; white powder all over the place. They don't notice her.)

MASSEY *(Anguished):* But I—

MARTÓN *(Hysterical):* The kind of money nobody-can-ever-touch-you-again-with! You do this thing and you'll never have to speak to a single person for the rest of your life, you'll be so rich! Ever!

(Massey cries out in confusion and frustration and temptation, an inchoate roar.)

HELEN: I thought what you wanted was to change your life.

(Pause. Massey turns to her. Dignified, as always, even with a nose white with blow.)

MASSEY: Hullo, Helen, my love. Shall I tell Nurse Carpaccio to bring us some tea? *(Beat. He smiles sadly. Caught. He shrugs)* I am trying, dear. This vile man next to me is Jeremiah Martón. We did our residency together at Skin Diseases. He's the cause of all this. You know I can't possibly afford this stuff anymore.

HELEN: Hey, kiddo, the last thing I want is a scene. I know how bored you get. I came to apologize for my father. I understand he came down here and, like, threatened you for money apparently.

MASSEY: It was quite an ugly scene, I'm afraid, my darling.

HELEN: I only came because I thought it might be productive, closure-wise, if we, clarification-wise, you know, kind of dealt with all of this, 'cause I'm riding a major bummer.

MARTÓN: Californian are you? Hullo. Sorry. Yes. Well.

HELEN: And you didn't like *my* people, Gray. Jeez.

MARTÓN *(Nasty):* Want a bit of this stuff? Doll like you, looks like you're not adverse to the stuff, is my guess, eh?

MASSEY *(Who has been standing still, de-animated):* Oh, don't be revolting, Martón.

HELEN: Gray, I know it's asking a lot, I know you hate it when I'm demanding, but could we—like—have a moment or something alone?

MARTÓN: I'll just take a bit of a tour through the place, and then I know this place in Malibu for Thai-Pesto Crostini, I'll treat as I've got these producers over the per diem barrel and I'm fucking them silly.

(He laughs and walks out. There is silence in his wake.)

MASSEY: He was rather a desperate case in London. Back then. Never invited to the right parties. A subject of mirth, gawky and earnest. Now he turns up, a handsome chap, about to self-destruct, intoxicated by you Yanks. So very sad, eh?

HELEN: He's a lot like you were, baby-boy, when you just got off the limey-boat, let me tell you.

(Helen lights them both a smoke. He declines.)

MASSEY: I suppose he is, isn't he. Yes. The dogs?

HELEN: Forget 'em. Fine. I drove down here to ask you a question. Something's been bothering me. Confusing me. When you upped and packed and walked out on me, I didn't say anything, you know? Slipping into wife-shock, nodding reasonably and letting you have your eloquent exit, Gray.

(She takes a breath. He looks concerned. She goes on.)

Forgive me, sorry, forgive me, it's taken me a few days to get the balls to come down here and see you, but I am madly pissed-off here.

MASSEY *(Nodding helpfully)*: Yes, no, marvelous. Let's talk about it, let's do. Hold all my calls. Go on.

HELEN: The thing that has been bothering me, and we know I have these major-self-worth problems (you always reminded me), but you helped me. I lost thirty-nine pounds during our marriage. And dad, who has all the sensitivity of a cloven hoof, always made me feel dumb, and then, you didn't, so I felt smart. But in retrospect, I was just taking your opinion of my intelligence on advisement, point being, in retrospect, that daddy was probably right. *(She smiles in apology, lips trembling. Controls herself)* Forgive me. This is a question I should've asked you were packing your Asprey bags—for two days I've been gorging myself on granola and anchovy paste, so I'm having trouble expressing, but the big question—and it's a two-parter. *(Beat)* Did you ever think I was smart?

MASSEY: Smart? Why of course I did! I still do! Smart? Christ. Yes!

HELEN: Because I'm not. I'm not. I'm . . . gutter. I'm not clever, you—God, making me read. Me! Throwing your books at me! And paintings! And ugh . . . God. Taste. You and your good taste. *(Beat)* You took me down with it, I couldn't talk, but—here's the second part of my question.

MASSEY: Go on, dear.

HELEN: Did you ever love me, Graydon?

MASSEY: Ah. Well. Love. Well. Yes. How could you ask that? With all my heart.

HELEN: But sweetheart. You see, I don't think I can believe you. I need to know. Did you ever love and respect me? Did you learn anything from me? Did I give you succor and warmth? What were you thinking when you hid in my chest at night, scared? Were we partners together? Did you ever stop in the middle of the goddamn day, Graydon, and wonder what I was doing or feeling? *(Pause)* Because I replay this thing in my head here and what I get to is that this marriage was a sad and—and—and decorous little affair—and what offends me—is that I do not believe you have answered me. I've had the last ten years of my life revealed to me as an absolute disaster. *(Beat)* If you know how much I hate myself for having let you lie to me for so long, I hate myself so much that it cancels out even blaming you. Oh, Graydon. Because what I've come up with is so interesting. And it never occurred to me consciously until this morning when I was eating my pasta. What I think is this: *(Pause)* I think you married me so as to become an American citizen.

MASSEY: Yes. It's true, of course, my darling.

HELEN *(Smiles)*: And yet I loved you, is the rub. So silly. It's like loving a machine that swallows heat and energy but does nothing at all. And, and—the only man I ever slept with. It's . . . crazy. To have loved like this. I am . . . curious, we know I'm a dumb JAP

blond, we know it but how do you sleep with someone for ten years? Wake up in the morning, the bad
breath, the smells, the life, someone who—basically—
bores you? *(Beat)* What—what is it that could make
you so dead inside that you could waste so much of
yourself? I just don't understand that.

MASSEY: I tried not to look at the thing . . . quite so . . .
closely, my love.

HELEN: And you fell in love with my father, my family, big,
larger than life broad-hipped robust American ethnics,
as you'd put it. "Kikes," as your friend would say.
(Beat) Not like those cold Dover Soles on Belgrave
Square, hunched over their abacuses, counting the take,
eh? No. We were alive and we held your interest.
(Beat) Irony. Irony. Because let me tell you, pal, if
daddy knew that you married me for citizenship he'd
have you dead the same day, I'm telling you, you'd be
killed. Don't you know us? Don't you know what he
is? If I told him there would be nothing anyone could
do to save you.

MASSEY: You couldn't possibly do that to me. I know you.

HELEN: You know the painting of the cat skeleton in your
parents' living room?

MASSEY: The George Stubbs, you mean?

HELEN: Yes.

MASSEY *(Contempt):* It's a dog.

HELEN: I want it. I've always wanted it. Think of it as this little girl's pound of flesh. If I don't get it, I'm telling you
here and now, I'll tell Hilly, and he'll have you decapi-
tated; they'll find your head in Encino behind the
Cineplex.

MASSEY: The *Stubbs*? Are you . . . mad? That's been pledged
to the Victoria and Albert for years! I can't just—what
do you expect me to do, have them pack it and Federal
Express it back to Malibu?

HELEN: You always find some charming little English way to
get whatever it is you crave, Gray. These are my terms.
In lieu of a reconciliation.

(Pause. Massey is staggered. He laughs.)

MASSEY: Did I just hear you say "in lieu of a reconciliation . . ."
HELEN: Yep.
MASSEY: You want to get back together? You just threatened to have me killed. Can't you make up your damn mind?
HELEN: It's just business with a little bitter love tossed in, hon. Think of me as Portia. Think of the pound of flesh. Just think.
MASSEY: I am totally speechless in the face of this monstrousness. I think it was Alexander Pope, Helen, who said, Civility is a jewel. A jewel. Please.
HELEN: Hey. Don't. Just don't. Not with me.
MASSEY: No.
HELEN: Graydon, how about this. Admit that somewhere deep down you've failed in your own game with yourself of exploitation and that you've loved me all along despite your basic shiftiness, maybe then you could accept my love.
MASSEY: Have you no self-respect at all?
HELEN *(With a sad, sweet smile):* Nope. None at all. You've taken it all out of me. *(Laughs)* I'm sorry Graydon. I'm not English. I can't do stiff upper lip. You were my only chance at a life. Now I'll be Hilly Lasker's old maid daughter of Beverly Hills and Malibu wandering madly down Rodeo Drive, years behind her time, forgetting all you taught me—about how to dress—doing charity work and getting fat again.
MASSEY: No, come on now, you've graduated therapy! Listen to yourself! Does that sound like you?
HELEN: Graduated? Huh! You were my shrink! I married you! This life of yours, Graydon, it has cost me dearly. And now—daddy's decided to go into politics—there's nothing for me but the life of a coastal commissioner's daughter, licking his stamps and answering his phones.
MASSEY: Your father's going into politics?
HELEN: He bought a seat on the coastal commission. He said he wanted to be in charge of passing water.
MASSEY: Despicable corrupt man. What a land this is.
HELEN: I gotta go. My cooking class meets tonight. We're doing fat-free blue corn souffles. It's time for you to

pay, Gray. The Stubbs. Or you. I'll wait for your word,
which I know has never been great.

(She exits. Massey sits, spent and stunned.)

MASSEY *(To himself, pacing):* This is exactly the type of business you adored, eh? Yes. In a nice white summer suit,
a pack of playing cards in your pocket. Fixed, no doubt,
marked. Always the cad, eh? And I did so adore that.
(Beat) I see you often, lately. A popinjay 'til the end,
breaking the bank at Monte Carlo and all, I do miss
you. You were so much fun for me. When you died,
you know, England meant nothing. Yes. A dull gray
bore. What is it you said to me? Your words of wis-
dom? "Never be earnest, never be dull, all be speedy,
lest your personality amount to null." Yes, that was it.
Always tricked your way out. Eh? *(Beat)* Always
tricked your way out. *(Massey pours himself a generous martini. Lights a cigar)* Dear father, wish I could
see you for a bit. Course, if I'd asked for help, you'd
say, "We're all grownups here, lad, we're all alone, my
boy . . ." *(Beat)* Pity, that. Eh? Ah and you, ending
your days at a corner table at Langan's, all alone with
your mixed grille. *(Beat)* Couldn't bear that for
myself. *(Beat. Simple. Dry. Bitter)* Course, you taught
me some good card tricks to slay 'em with and I'm a
fine . . . juggler thanks to you. That's something, eh?

Scene Three

*There is a silence. The light changes. Sunset
descending behind the smog-stunted palms of
San Pedro. Massey, at Toffler's bed, unwrapping
the bandage about his neck.*

TOFFLER: I know all these people who've died, it's always the
same story, but I've learned one thing; if you want to
live, it helps if you've got a reason. Something to look
to.

MASSEY *(Barely listening, unwrapping):* Um, quite, hold still stop moving about it only makes it worse, please.

TOFFLER: A list. That's what I'm saying, I thought I'd make a list, what do you think of that, doctor? Of reasons to live. A rigorous, unsentimental, list of things worth hanging in for.

MASSEY: I hate sentimentality myself.

TOFFER: But, you know, all the really good reasons are totally sentimental, so, bummer. Anyway, given the choice, I'd rather not die from my treatment! Okay?

MASSEY: Oh, these pricks in radiation've really burnt you up pretty bad, haven't they?

TOFFLER *(Anguished, lashes out):* Hey, I can't even eat, okay. *(Beat)* Which, fine, is a blessing, the swill they hand out here, so I'm better off. Did you know I was a chef in civilian life?

MASSEY: Civilian?

TOFFLER: I'm now such an insider that I think of the healthy as civilians.

MASSEY: Toffler, the burns do heal. They tell me. I won't testify to that, I'm still finding my sea legs, but they heal, and list or not, you'll live.

TOFFLER: Well now I can just lay my head back and rest, at ease.

MASSEY *(Frustrated):* But why have you come to this clinic? I smell the money on you, you're a rich kid gone bad.

TOFFLER: It takes one to know one, doesn't it pal.

MASSEY: Why haven't your people taken you back in and put you at a real hospital. This is a charnel house, really. Could I talk to your family? If they saw this place . . . ? Surely . . . ?

TOFFLER: I really have no other option. This is it, Massey. When—when I told you I've lived badly—I meant it. Listen to me, pal—I have hurt people.

MASSEY: Yes but you've done good things too—you took care of your friend when he was dying.

TOFFLER: I thought he'd leave me his money. Which he ended up giving to the Nature Conservancy and Earth First, the prick. Not even good causes.

MASSEY: Oh my, you *have* been a nasty piece of work, haven't you?

TOFFLER: Basically, I've run a confidence racket since I was eight or nine.

MASSEY: Really, a con-artist?

TOFFLER: I took all my friends, "investors" in a little cafe. All my friends, for dope money, *Comme Des Garçons* money, Armani and Pesto cash, ripped off people who couldn't bear up, who've suffered significantly in my wake, yes, fucked people. Without a condom, literally and figuratively, pal. Stole from my parents beyond forgiveness. *(Beat)* Why? I know how many slumlords and dictators get off for nothing, but maybe, when you're alone at the very end, and after, maybe it's then at the end that it all comes out in the wash.

MASSEY: I don't know, myself, I can't say.

TOFFLER: You must have an opinion, the nurse outside says you were a psychiatrist.

MASSEY: Oh, did she? Really. You probably ate badly and lived too close to electrical lines and toxic dumps or come from a dubious gene pool, but let me tell you one thing, even as a shrink, when they started going on about good and evil, I had to hit myself to stay awake.

TOFFLER: I have no one else to talk to, I would prefer someone less like me, given the choice, believe me.

MASSEY: What was on your list of reasons to live?

TOFFLER: Very small. Pathetic. Flirting in restaurants. A particular painting, a Balthus that I like. The tunnel onto Pacific Coast Highway—when you're suddenly at the beach.

(Beat. He stops, miserable.)

MASSEY: Such a short list, Jonathon.

TOFFLER: I am sick of myself, doctor.

MASSEY *(A smile):* I must go, I do have other patients.

(Beat. Toffler makes a move. It hurts very badly.)

Do you require more pain pills.

TOFFLER: No. That, I do not. Because I'm finally feeling something.

(Martón enters, sunglasses on.)

MARTÓN: Oh *here you are.* Thai. Pesto. *Linguini.* Malibu. Now. Come on. *(Beat)* This Toffler's a marvelous patient.

MASSEY *(Smiles):* Oh, you've met? *(Beat. Rueful)* Would you look in on him for me for the next twenty-four hours, I'm off to London.

MARTÓN: London? But what for, Graydon?

MASSEY: For money, Jeremiah. For money.

(Massey exits, slamming door. Martón reacts.)

ACT TWO

Scene One

The house must be a surprise. Where one expects antiques, it is, in fact, the most postmodern architectural furniture. Angles abound.

Jocelyn Massey, a woman in her fifties, quite stunning, dressed in Ungaro finery, sits with martini in hand. Swifty, Lord Kitterson, her brother-in-law, stands by the huge window overlooking the square. He wears an extraordinarily expensive suit, say a Comme Des Garçons or one of the Japanese. A Yoji. Massey enters and is astonished by what he sees. He sighs in relief, as above the fireplace is, indeed, a rather wonderful George Stubbs painting of a dog skeleton. Massey is unnoticed for a moment.

JOCELYN: Yes, that's when I said to those pricks, if you think I'm going to leverage on a fucking cannery, a *sprat* cannery in bloody *Lisbon*, you're mad. . . . You're starkers.

SWIFTY: Why can't all those little people just go and blow themselves up? That's what I want to know. Why not? And leave us be? Well? Why?

JOCELYN: There's nobody left to play with in the world, anymore, is there? No, we're all alone, Swifty, Lord Kitterson . . . *(She stops, having noticed Massey)* Oh dear. Oh my. Oh shit.

SWIFTY: Oh dear God in heaven—he's back.

MASSEY: Hullo, mummy. Hullo Uncle Swifty, Lord Kitterson.

JOCELYN: Did you bring your wife?

MASSEY: It's all finished, we've split. It's all over. Everything, it's all over.

JOCELYN: I see you've acquired that particularly annoying American trait of "just dropping in."

MASSEY: I wanted to give you a surprise. I don't know why, but I thought you might be happy to see me, after so many years . . .

SWIFTY *(Mixes Massey a stiff one):* Don't be ridiculous, lad, of course we're happy. Don't mind your mother, tried to take over a shipping line in Lisbon and the bloody, bloody, bloody, bloody Koreans came swooping down like . . . well, dare I say it, yellow-tailed-howler-monkeys and made off with the things, tricky little chinky-buggers! Specialized in smoked sardines in tomato sauce too.

(Swifty staggers drunkenly out.)

JOCELYN: Happy? Happy to see you? Of course I'm happy. What mother would not be happy to see her boy after so long? What mother? No. A beast perhaps. Tell me, do you still have an American passport?

MASSEY *(Smiles, shakes his head):* The house looks so different.

JOCELYN: Yes, it does, doesn't it? Do you like it? Just trying to fight the blahs. Well, it was the same for—what was it—last couple of hundred years, I think. But when your father died . . . *(Pause. She smiles, shakes her head)* When your father . . . *died* . . . you know he died, don't you? We did, I believe . . . exchange cards then . . . oh, I'm not sure, there were so many of them. When your father died. Yes. *(Beat)* The *Times* had a lovely piece, didn't even mention any scandals with the exchequery, so long ago, one lives in the past, eh? *(Beat)* When your father died, yes, we redecorated. So many hundreds of years of mustiness, and Swifty and I sat here, and he said to me, "An Empire Chair has no place in the modern world." I thought that quite true. Don't you? I thought it perceptive. Got rid of all the silly little Chippendale. Well, once—your father died—

MASSEY *(Patient):* Mother—

JOCELYN: My. Look at you. Your face has lines. Your eyes are so hard. Has America done that to you? Taken your youth?

MASSEY: Within a matter of days. Los Angeles is a sort of huge, smoggy, reverse Fountain of Youth. Ponce De Leon would have keeled over after his first lunch. *(Beat)* I have done myself in, Jocelyn.

JOCELYN: Poor boy. Yes! Yes, I knew there'd come this day. Yes. Have you finally managed to wreck your life with your calculating? Yes?

MASSEY: I am in need of a sum of money.

JOCELYN *(Closes her eyes and smiles, nodding)*: Of course. Yes. Have you seen, driving up, what they've done to the Square? It's hardly a park anymore, the flowers are miserly, yes? I go in there myself once or twice a day, kick the wogs out and replant the lilies where they've pissed on 'em. Go in there with my brolly. There was a piece on me in the *Times*, "Wife of corrupt Tory suicide kicks homeless out of Belgrave Square." Big laughingstock, don't imagine you'd seen it, out in Malibu. But I said "I have a right to a lifestyle, I have a right to pretty things about me!" *(Beat. She sobs)* "I have a right!" That, of course, is the language of the poor. "I have a right." But . . . *(She opens the huge window. The snow swirls down)* I do love that park.

MASSEY: Mother, I am here in desperation. I am here placing myself at your mercy. A quality which has never taxed you abundantly, to be sure. But I will be killed unless I pay off my father-in-law a sum of money. I shall be gunned down in the streets, I tell you, like a mad dog.

JOCELYN *(After a moment)*: Go on . . .?

MASSEY *(Laughs)*: What do you mean "Go on?" God, I've missed you, mum, who else can negotiate like this, eh? This is the bottom line, my dear: Hilly Lasker will ice me! I've been caught out!

JOCELYN: And?

MASSEY *(Rueful but enjoying this)*: Well I'll die, I'm afraid. Is this something you need to consider?

JOCELYN: Depends on how much you're asking for.

MASSEY: My, you are a specimen. Jocelyn, the Gorgon of Belgravia, watch her devour her young, bury her husband, marry her brother-in-law, I'm telling you, it's like walking into a bad church guild players' version of *Hamlet.*

JOCELYN: Money. Isn't it extraordinary? Let them kill you, and you'll finally have learned the truth about the Americans, you'll say "Mother was right." *(Lost in reverie)* What would your father have done, seeing you in this state, aged and threadbare to look at, unshaven and hungry, drenched and smelly—

MASSEY: I most certainly am not smelly, mother.

JOCELYN: You reek of failure! We sent you out into the world, ahhh and you . . . oh, listen to me go on, I'm boring myself. How much do they want?

MASSEY: One point five million.

JOCELYN: Pounds or dollars?

MASSEY: Pounds.

JOCELYN: Fuck.

MASSEY: One mil in cash, five hundred at the bank of Commerce, Smoke and Mirrors in Lucerne.

JOCELYN: Give up your American passport.

MASSEY: Done.

JOCELYN: Come back to the Church, confession and all.

MASSEY: It's a deal.

JOCELYN: Move back to London.

MASSEY: Oh God.

JOCELYN: Back into the house.

(Massey nods.)

MASSEY: Yes.

JOCELYN: And become engaged to Lady Hammersmith-Urbaine-Supton-Stoat.

(Pause. Massey drinks.)

MASSEY: You are to the male genitalia, mother, what Christian Barnard is to the heart. *(A moan)* Why Stoaty? I mean, anyone but The Stoat. Why her?

JOCELYN: Her family's got shipping yards I want in Southampton.

MASSEY: I see. And then, is it safe to say I may divorce her after you get your shipping lines?

JOCELYN: Unless they've something else I want.

MASSEY: You strike a hard bargain, mother.

JOCELYN: Yes, and you give away too much without a fight.

MASSEY: Well, here we are then.

JOCELYN: Yes. Here we are. Fancy that. The Lloyds man'll bring the money 'round tomorrow. Ring for Tellman to bring you some supper. I must retire now, Swifty may have some news of the Panamanian shipping lines. Good night my son, I love you very much.

(She is gone. Massey looks out at the glorious snowbound night.)

MASSEY: Cheers. Won again. *(He looks up, smiles. He picks up the telephone)* Yes, Tellman, it's Master Graydon here. I do hope I haven't awakened you. Would you mind very much bringing me a lamb sandwich and a glass of stout? *(Beat)* No, I'm not in *Los Angeles*, I'm *upstairs*. Good. Yes. *(He hangs up, looks out at the snow. He toasts himself)* Jesus.

(Swifty darts drunkenly in.)

SWIFTY: Your mother just told me the good news, always knew you'd end up back here, eh? Damn good. Well, my gift to you—a shipping line—we just procured the bugger—Panno-Anglo-Suez-Oceanic, and we're putting it in your name, congratulations and sorry for the inconvenience but best if you camp out here tonight; your old room's an office and faxes come in all night, dreadful clatter, more comfortable, I should imagine, if you don't really mind and can bear it for now if you just slept on the sofa. Soon set up old digs for you, just like before, pictures of Noddy on the wall and naughty photos under the bed, eh? *(Beat)* You're a shipping magnate now, boy! G'night. For some reason, it gets awfully cold in here. This should help. It was your dad's.

(He tosses Massey a pair of flannel pajamas and exits, but not before grabbing a bottle from the drinks tray. Massey undresses and puts them on. An old red-and-white broad stripe, somewhat hinting at a prison uniform.)

MASSEY *(Sniffs the pajamas as he puts them on):* Ah, father, they even smell of you. Your cologne, a special blend. Like fermenting lemon rind from last night's gin martini, eh? Precisely the aroma. And here it is—that smell! And how long've you been gone, you old crook? Ages, eh? So how is it that your scent remains so close? *(Beat)* Father. Did you feel this way? So hard to preserve your lifestyle, so much work to keep all the balls up in the air, eh? Why does it take so much work? Ah, that smell, so dry, powdery . . . that's what memory is, isn't it, dad? A small scent. You loved being a cad. Cads and bounders, you and I, eh?

(He sits down on the sofa. He covers himself with a blanket and looks out at the snow. Young Graydon enters wearing a disheveled uniform— that of a Fifth Former perhaps at Eton. Massey, in his pajamas, becomes Sterling Massey, Gray's dad.)

STERLING: Graydon, lad, how are you? Been kicked out of school again? Good boy. Ah.

YOUNG MASSEY: You wanted to see me?

STERLING: Did you come down by train? I always carry, when I'm on a train trip, a pack of good playing cards.

YOUNG MASSEY: Yes, I should imagine you would, pa.

STERLING: You know why, laddie?

YOUNG MASSEY: I should imagine it's 'cause you can always pick up a couple of pounds that way, if you mark 'em right.

STERLING: Exactly the point. You want to thicken the blacks with a bit of gouache paint, not even as much as a nail clipping from your pinky. End up pounds richer. They'll never know. Mind you, only do it while traveling. Never a regular game, if they caught you, your crowd, they'd keelhaul you.

YOUNG MASSEY: Of course, father.

STERLING *(Slightly slurred with gin)*: The point is, what I mean about traveling, Gray, is—leave here. It's all dead here. For a man like . . . us. Men like me and you, there's no room. Your mother says you're thinking of . . . America?

YOUNG MASSEY: California. Yes. It's bound to be somewhat more—

STERLING *(Cuts him off)*: No doubt about it, it's bound to be

more . . . *(He shrugs)* Home's hell, eh? The Inferno,
isn't it? Read your Dante?

YOUNG GRAY: Yes. You gave me your old copy.

STERLING: I feel like London's gone Dante on me.

*(Sterling weeps quietly, wipes his eyes and nose
with pajama sleeve.)*

YOUNG GRAY: I'm very sorry, father.

STERLING: You'll be fine if you think of it all as—as—as a
chess game. Life. A chess game with yourself, and
think of all the others as pawns in this game with
yourself, you'll be fine. It's good that you leave, that
you want to travel. You know, I'm an *old* crook, and
your mother's a chilly creature and my brother's been
fucking her. *(Beat)* He's going to set me up to take a
fall for him, he's always played at the drunken buffoon
but he's Claudius, he's dangerous. So don't come back
here, lad. They've no affection for you. Let's say *goodbye* here—now. And go to America and don't come
back here, don't ring up. You remind your mother too
much of me, you see, and she'll set out to destroy you.
(Beat) Let's say . . . *goodbye* then and never ring one
another, not even when we're blue, 'cause we'll only
get into trouble. I do wish I could . . . give you some
money, but your mother's . . . *(Beat)* You've turned
into a damn good kid. But don't turn into too much of
a thief, eh? A little bit crooked's fine, but greedy's
beneath us. Piss off. *(Beat)* Gray. You know, we never
tell our—I've never said that I love you, I despise that
type of language. Matinee talk.

*(Beat. The snow swirls down. Tellman, the butler,
enters with tray. A plate of olives, some crackers,
an apple and a beer. Young Gray slips out of the
room.)*

TELLMAN: Sir, are you all right? You were talking to yourself.
We've no sandwiches and I can't send out for any. All
the shops're closed. We've only olives. But we did have
a ginger beer.

MASSEY: Hullo Tellman, so very nice to see you.

TELLMAN: You were talking to yourself, sounded just like your father, thought he was back.

MASSEY: Just jet lag is all.

TELLMAN: Are you sleeping in here? It gets cold. I could make you a fire?

MASSEY: I'll be just fine.

TELLMAN: *(Whispers):* Your uncle turns the heat off. Doesn't like to spend the money. I tell you, it's all gone bad since the old man passed on, Master Gray. *(He turns to Massey, imploring)* You're not going to stay, are you? I only stay on waiting to get paid. They promise they'll pay me, but they never do. I'm owed back pay for seven years. Used to be, being a servant was a *joy* in this world, in this country—nothing better. But now you have to fight for your life. They have money! Yes! But they don't spend it on *life* like your father used to. It's all business and faxes and Federal Express and clocks and phones and Xeroxes and Arabs and Latins and funny smells and you can't get *food* on the table anymore because they don't honor our accounts anywhere, not even Fortnums, this isn't the way life was meant to be for people like us, Master Gray! I often think of the way this house lit up with you and your aged pa playing cards night and day and the *laughter.* *(Beat)* So what if he brought whores home? *(Beat)* Was that any reason for your mother to be so very . . . *cruel* to him? When he was in gaol, even though it was only a period of months, she never visited him! And it broke him, knowing what was going on here.

(Beat. Tellman shuffles out.)

MASSEY: Dear God in heaven. Dear God. Please.

(Jocelyn enters. Her hair is down. She is in her dressing gown. She carries a spade and bucket. She has on a heavy, fur-lined overcoat.)

JOCELYN: I can't sleep.

MASSEY: Ah. *(Beat)* I've some pills . . .

JOCELYN *(A bitter laugh):* Oh I'm sure you *do.*

MASSEY: What do you mean by that?

JOCELYN *(Sorrowful):* How could I trust you? How could I trust such people?

MASSEY: For heaven's sake, what do you think I'd do to you? Mother?

JOCELYN *(Scornful):* "Pills." Was that what you did all day? Eh? *(Beat. Fury)* So they won't notice it all falling apart around them? Gave them pills, did you? Why would I want your pills? Belgrave Square looks like a burnt-out lot, a marsh! At least *I do* something! *(Looks down at the bucket)* Plant flowers. And then, occasionally—there's something lovely to look at out the window and one is reminded of what it's meant to be here. So thank you, no, I'll not take your pills and shirk my duties in a fog which is exactly what you want!

MASSEY: I can assure you that's hardly the case. I merely wanted to be . . . helpful.

JOCELYN: If you want to be helpful, you'll come out into the Square with me and help with these gladiolas.

MASSEY: Now? It's snowing. It's two in the morning.

JOCELYN: I'm perfectly aware of the hour. I'm an insomniac, not an idiot.

(Jocelyn says nothing, shakes her head, and exits. Massey stands for a moment, puts on his overcoat over the pajamas and exits with his mother into the snowy London night.)

Scene Two

The verandah overlooking Belgrave Square. Morning. Massey and Lady Hammersmith-Urbaine-Supton-Stoat. She is eating a cream-laden scone.

STOAT: When your mother rang up this morning at dawn, I smiled before I picked up. I always knew we'd end up together. The fact is, I suspected always that I would eventually have you once you got over your dread of intimacy. Your passion for street life. Oh, yes, you and your pa, looking for scullery maids together. . . . Yes.

MASSEY: Yes, you always were a bit of a soothsayer, Stoaty. Remember we used to all call you that?

STOAT: Yes, I knew I was the subject of mirth for you and your smart set. Your nervous little Tattler-back-page-spread set, yes. Equestrian Girls from Green Park roaring at Stoat. *(Beat)* But now your mother has you cornered. You've run out of steam.

MASSEY: My dear girl, it's jet lag is all.

STOAT: No. I know that bored bleary-eyed look, glazed halibut eyes peering out at me. I even know what you're doing, the Massey sociopath trick, looking for my weak spot.

MASSEY: Not at all.

STOAT: Well my weak spot's my strength. Oh the fantasies I've had of being held down by you; your unshaven face rubbing against my thigh—this dream I've had of eroding your indifference and—here we are. Here we are!

MASSEY: My God, you are in an icy woman! How'd you get so clever?

STOAT: The fact is, we are equals, you and I. And our marriage need not be despicable even though you are driven to it by having finally been cornered, ruined and needy.

MASSEY: This business of having to make up for lost time has turned all the women in my life into men!

STOAT *(Laughs):* Yes! Precisely that! Suffering fools, being laughed at, yes. Despising my class, loathing my brothers off to Baliol, milky flabby skins and upturned noses. Yes! Proper pairs of shoes, waiting at home. Name it, it is sufficient to say that my life chilled me— but—Graydon Massey of Belgrave Square, I always knew—one day, I would have. Like it or not.

MASSEY: How extraordinary, darling. To be so dead set certain of something in the face of all reality, and yet, to hope and persist. Isn't that remarkable?

STOAT: Yes but don't you agree that reality is the great destroyer, Graydon? If I were realistic, I'd never get out of bed.

MASSEY: But what if you end up with nothing? Living this

way? On the edge of a kind of madness, love? The life you describe, it's a rum affair. The waiting for a phone call . . .

STOAT: Been my pleasure.

(Pause. Massey smiles.)

MASSEY: Well. Another marriage of convenience for me, eh? What about passion? What about that? Seems a *distant* pleasure to me now.

STOAT: Passion. Poor, poor Gray. So transparent, so full of hope, despite your thievery and petty American psychiatric deceptions. Some advice: Let the English chill you feel about you in this room overtake you.

MASSEY: I shall never give you what you want, Stoaty. Understand: I'll be reduced to flare-ups, booze-ups, affairs, money-laundering schemes, sneak-offs to Paris and a dotage spent gardening by myself. I'll shut you out, never love you, you're doomed.

STOAT: Don't really give a shittez-vous, darling, between you, me, and the lamppost.

MASSEY *(Polite and confused):* Er, pardon?

STOAT: Yes, quite. But you see, my love is fueled by your despising me. If you turned, I'd lose interest before the first kind word.

(Swifty joins them, dressed as if ready for an appearance on MTV as guest V.J.)

SWIFTY *(Hands Massey a leather satchel):* Morning, darlings, here's your money, go pay off the nasty blighter and to the devil with him, eh? Nasty business, go on with leading decent lives again, pick up where we left off, eh? Hello, Stoaty, off your feed? Look less swollen than usual.

MASSEY: Tell mother goodbye for me, will you, Swifty. I must get to Heathrow, back in a week or so, got a patient going through a bit of a rough patch just now, want to see him through.

STOAT: Why a week?

MASSEY: Because, your ladyship, within the week, with any luck, he should be dead.

STOAT: Dead? How stimulating to work with dead people. Are they interesting?

SWIFTY: Burma. Lots of dead people there. Some quite fascinating too.

(Massey lifts the Stubbs off the wall, turns to exit. Jocelyn is standing in the doorway wearing an old pale nightgown, her hair down—she is older than we thought.)

JOCELYN *(Looks at Massey with sadness, smiles):* All of us are getting older, Graydon. That is the only inevitability and what will we have to say when we can barely speak at the end?

MASSEY *(Hard):* You might ask yourself that question, mother, rather than me.

JOCELYN: Ahh, you have such an appetite. So voracious, Graydon. The Massey touch. You are too young for forgiveness and I am too old for kindness.

MASSEY: I can assure you, dear lady, I'm not as hungry as I once was.

(He makes a futile attempt to hide the painting. Jocelyn waves her hand.)

JOCELYN *(Weary):* Take it. Take it. What use have I for it?

(Massey turns to leave. He gingerly kisses Jocelyn as he passes her. She steels herself. He exits. There is silence in his wake.)

SWIFTY: Good. Always hated that damn picture. Damn stupid drawing if you ask me. What good's a cat without flesh and fur, eh?

STOAT *(Sipping tea):* It's a question I've asked myself many times, Swifty, Lord Kitterson, but alas there's no answer.

SWIFTY: Probably the whole point, my dear, isn't it? Probably the whole *entire* point!

JOCELYN *(Turns and looks out the window at the park and sighs):* The fucking gollywogs are out in full force today, aren't they? Probably dug up my gladioli all over the place, damn them. *(She calls outside)* Go

away! You've no right to be in Belgrave Square, damn
you! Oh . . . *(She stops, shaking her head)* Nothing to
be done, is there? Nothing.

STOAT: Seems we've run out of the gooseberry marmalade.
Tellman! *Tellman!*

(Blackout.)

Scene Three

*Lights up on Massey's office at the clinic. Martón
sits at the desk, book in hand. It is terribly hot
and the fan is on high. He is sweating, drenched.
Massey enters carrying the satchel and the
Stubbs.*

MARTÓN *(Reading aloud):*
Ah, love, let us be true
To one another! for the world, which seems
To lie before us like a land of dreams,
So various, so beautiful, so new . . .

MASSEY:
Hath really neither joy, nor love, nor light,
Nor certitude, nor peace . . . nor . . .

(Massey struggles to remember)

. . . nor help for pain . . . ;
And we are here as on a darkling plain
Swept with confused alarms of struggle and flight,
Where ignorant armies clash by night.
—Dover Beach. Matthew Arnold.

MARTÓN: And was it productive for you there, across the
pond? How *is* dreary old Londontown? Where ignorant armies clash by night.

MASSEY: Genuinely sad. Hadn't quite realized. It all seemed
so gussied up. Dolled up. Tarted up. Painted faces. But
underneath . . . *(He shakes his head. Beat)* In Beverly
Hills there was a certain type who used to come to me.
Very old. Ancient. Pots of cash. And something quite
spoilt just under the surface. Under the skin. Which

had been stretched taut. You know? That impossible
blond hair on a seventy-nine-year-old.

MARTÓN: London. Yes. I understand.

MASSEY: Toffler?

MARTÓN: This heatwave has just about done him in. If there
were air conditioning. But he's in dreadful shape. He
refuses painkillers.

MASSEY: You were kind to look in on him.

MARTÓN: You know, it's poverty that's killing him. What
could you have been thinking when you thought you
could do any good at a place like this? Even if you
wanted to suffer, surely suffering somewhere where
you're of some value, where you can have an effect
would be more to the point of whatever—*transaction*
you've made with yourself?

MASSEY: I have been doing some—reevaluating. I've thought
about your offer.

*(He opens the satchel, which literally glows green
with all the money.)*

MARTÓN: Good Lord, yes. My. How much?

MASSEY: Well. There's a million dollars. The motion picture
business, you know, so exhilarating.

(Massey tosses satchel to Martón.)

MARTÓN *(Smiles):* You're such a tortured man, Gray. Back
and forth, agonized and contorted and here you finally
are, come 'round with a cool mil. Oh Gray. At the end
of the day, being rich makes you so very wealthy.

MASSEY: You really are in your element, aren't you?

MARTÓN: Well I certainly won't apologize for adjusting to
the modern sensibility after having spent my life as a
boy scout, no. *(Beat)* Congratulations. You're now a
film producer with Fiasco Films. Our logo is "It's a
Fiasco!" How does it feel? Dear, dear Gray?

MASSEY: I'm starting to feel like I'm getting on my feet!

MARTÓN: It's a super feeling, isn't it? Well. I'd best be off,
there's so many partners in this venture, it's important
to reinvest quickly or there'll be no room.

MASSEY: Big business, is it?

MARTÓN: Fortune Fucking Five Hundred, mate, and growing every day. Graydon. You know, it's marvelous, the best part of this, for me, is being able to help my friends—help someone like you.

BRACKETT *(Entering):* Doctor, someone's vomited in the hall. Mind you don't slip.

MARTÓN: I'll get on it right away.

(Satchel in hand, he is gone, dancing a little jig. Massey stands alone in the heat of his office, the Stubbs leans on a chair.)

BRACKETT: How nice of you to come back, Doctor Massey.

MARTÓN *(Offstage):* Fuck!

MASSEY *(Mild):* If you would remember to knock, perhaps I'd—

BRACKETT *(Cuts this off):* Who? Who do you think you are? What—what do you think we're doing here? You lout. These people are dying.

MASSEY *(Angry):* Yes! Needlessly!

BRACKETT: Is that why you walked out? Hey. Hey. What is this? Am I fuckin' nuts or something? Because I don't get it. You came here. You said you'd spent five years in Beverly Hills, and that you felt useless, you needed to help. This is how you help?

MASSEY: Are you quite finished?

BRACKETT: Just empty out your desk, please. While I'm here. I want to watch. Boy. Guys like you make me laugh. Man. What good have you done for anybody?

MASSEY: And do you imagine, you self-righteous, impotent little do-gooder, that you've ever been of any assistance to any of these people? Because this isn't a hospital—*nothing works!* In a real hospital, people come in sick and leave better. In a real hospital, someone can get a splint, an aspirin, a band-aid. In a real hospital, there are stitches. In a real hospital, there are orderlies. Not rivers of plasma and vomit and just three Trinidadian residents who can't tell the difference between measles, smallpox, and sarcoma. So please don't lecture me on being here until you find a way to run this place competently! Instead of lording over the sick so as to feel better as they pop off. You're worse than I am, lady, because you know *precisely* what you're doing and—even more—contemptibly—you know what you *should* be doing. Which makes you nothing so much as a ghoulish little commandant, Dr. Mengele's book-keeper!

(Pause.)

BRACKETT: You don't hold back, do you?

MASSEY: I could go on, believe me. I find you beneath contempt, really.

BRACKETT: I'm not wild about you, either, pal.

MASSEY: Well. There we are.

(Beat.)

BRACKETT: Is that a Stubbs? *(She looks at the painting carefully)* This is a real George Stubbs?

MASSEY *(Cautious):* Yes. Yes it is. Why? That's exactly what it is.

BRACKETT: It's so great.

MASSEY: Uhm. Yes, it is . . . duckie. You like it? Do you? Brackett?

BRACKETT: It breaks my heart in two that a despicable little fop like you should possess such a thing. A waste.

MASSEY: Uhm.

BRACKETT: Oh I've always had a flame for Stubbs. I went to London twenty-four years ago and I saw "A Comparative Anatomical Exposition of the Structure of the Human Body with that of a Tiger and a Common Fowl." We're so different. And he made that clear, but the same too. The same. And—and exquisite—all. Even his realization, in the painting of a horse—say—of the preoccupations of a dying class. There we all are. In the painting. *(She smiles)* My husband. He took me. He started this place. But he died. He'd have hated you. Taken you out into the courtyard and thrashed you to within an inch of your life then prayed over your broken body and wept. That was him. You'd have adored him. *(Brackett pours herself a drink and lights a smoke. She looks out the window at San Pedro's twinkling lights)* That painting has the scent of my husband. Too bad. Decent man. Decent man. What a time. None left. I wasn't much of anything before I met my husband and I'm pretty thinned out without him, but he was decent. *(She turns to Massey, imploring)* Why is that so impossible to ask for in any one now? Why is that, doctor? Why is it that nothing . . . works? We all know it—you're quite right, you know. I feel so proud of myself for sticking it out down here. Every time one of them dies, Graydon . . . I feel stronger. Isn't that horrible? Every time one of them dies, I feel like one of those women on the prairie, moving out west, being brave. Ugly. So ugly . . . *(Beat)* Is wanting to help people so silly?

MASSEY: Perhaps. It's *expecting* something for it that's so . . .

(He shrugs and grimaces. Pours himself a drink. There is a moment between them. She looks at the Stubbs.)

BRACKETT: Breaks my heart, seeing this painting.

MASSEY *(Tired, a sigh):* Well then take it as payment for Toffler.

BRACKETT: Oh it's a priceless masterpiece. Payment for a *patient?*

MASSEY: Sell it. Fix the place up. Buy things. Do something. Take the painting.

BRACKETT *(Astonished):* Doctor Massey, what kind of man are you?

MASSEY: I'm a tired one, right now, Brackett. One condition. I stay until the end for Toffler. Is that acceptable to you? I should not imagine it'll be very long for him and in the meantime I'll keep out of trouble.

BRACKETT *(Touched):* But don't ignore the rest of your duties. The others worked double shifts while you were out tom-catting around town and whoring all over east L.A. most likely. And then . . . we can perhaps talk about your position here . . .

MASSEY: No, you're right. I don't belong here. A fop doing penance, sloppy and unfelt.

BRACKETT *(She picks up the painting):* You didn't by any chance steal it, did you?

MASSEY *(Amused):* My great, great, I think great grandfather commissioned it. The dog was his. Mauled a poacher. Only his glove left. Still got it.

BRACKETT: Just wanted to make certain. *(Exits)*

Scene Four

Massey stands at his desk, then walks out to the ward. Toffler's bed. He is asleep.

MASSEY: So dreadful. To die alone. Isn't it? Not the way it is meant to end, for anyone, life. *(He shakes his head)* What of your family? What sort of people don't forgive? To say . . . *goodbye.* Maybe that's their revenge. Quietly . . . surviving us. Going on. Is this what you come to? A life without friends ending somewhere ghastly? And what to come? My father. His lone death. Released from Brixton Prison, came home, to what? Went to Langan's Brasserie for lamb chops and a beer and then put a gun under his ear at the elephant cage at the Regents Park Zoo, snuck in at midnight. *(Quietly angry)* What of that quiet death?

(He sits down in the chair beside Toffler and takes his hand, and falls asleep. Lights fade.)

Scene Five

Morning. Massey wanders, disheveled, into his office. Martón is sitting in his chair. He is wearing a marvelous Japanese suit of aggressive color.

MARTÓN: Graydon, dear boy, we are quite, quite rich.

MASSEY: How marvelous! Already?

MARTÓN: I simply bought low and sold high, really, it's just banking, the way we do it. We're a *film studio.* You're worth, I should say, well, about thirteen point three million dollars.

MASSEY: Good Lord. What an odd tingly feeling.

MARTÓN: And of course, it keeps coming. I've been looking at offices. Columbia offered us a production deal. They saw the rough cut of my AIDS picture, flipped! We're legit. Course, I have to check with the other partners . . .

MASSEY: Who *are* these other partners?

MARTÓN: Well. It's very tricky, you see, but there's a little film studio in Surrey, Hammersmith-Urbaine-Supton-Stoat Studios? Did horror films in the Fifties, remember?

MASSEY: Hammersmith-Urbaine-Supton-Stoat. Yes. Indeed. I do. Really? How . . . marvelous.

MARTÓN: And we have an arrangement with a very genteel little shipping line out of London docks. Outfit called Anglo-Panno-Something-Oceanic. Nice firm.

MASSEY: That wouldn't be Panno-Anglo-Suez-Oceanic, you mean?

MARTÓN: Oh, you've *heard* of them, then, have you?

MASSEY *(Smiling):* I think I read something somewhere.

MARTÓN: Then there's this chap on the California coastal commission with whom there's an arrangement.

MASSEY: Oh, really? How . . . convenient for us.

MARTÓN: Yes, and he can find out all the Coast Guard operation plans as well as Customs and DEA schedules for San Pedro Harbor where he also just happens to own a fruit and veggie wholesale warehouse, handy for storage. Lasker-Big Fruit Co.

(Beat.)

MASSEY: And, ah, who runs the whole thing?

MARTÓN: That's the odd thing. It seems to run itself. I sometimes feel like a cog in a wheel. A woman in London and some Koreans, I think. We don't know for sure.

MASSEY: Isn't it extraordinary how, in this country, things can just turn so very quickly. You can go right to the bottom of the pond and then find yourself . . . chief . . . catfish . . .

MARTÓN *(Insanely exhilarated):* Yes! Yes! But you see, now

I can tell you, this grueling charade we've both been keeping up, let's drop it!

MASSEY: Charade?

MARTÓN: None of this means a thing without you. That's why I sought you out. Look—with such money we can live like kings. Together. Two kings. Two queens.

MASSEY *(Aghast):* Good God, Jeremiah, please. No, you've simply got the wrong idea.

MARTÓN: Oh no, no, no, no. No, no, no, no. Don't. *Spare me* "wrong idea." You've had dreadful relationships with women, you dress too well to be straight, your mother was domineering and your dad remote, you want me as much as I want you! We can have it all!

MASSEY: You've got the wrong idea, really, I don't mind that . . . er . . . lifestyle, as . . . repugnant as I personally, happen to er . . . find it . . . but . . . *(Pause)* Jeremiah. It's not for me.

MARTÓN: Which lifestyle is that? Being in love—is that what's not for you?

MASSEY: I resent that.

MARTÓN: Well, name me one thing or person you've ever loved.

MASSEY: So, excuse me. Please explain this to me. Because I don't think that I'm quite up to speed. You've done all this for love?

MARTÓN: Yes.

MASSEY: So all of the dope dealing, the cocaine and all. It's all for love is it? I'm sure all the shaking crack addicts in the corridor here would appreciate the great irony of your deep love for me and all that it's done for them. No, Jeremiah, I find this notion of love you're talking about just a bit too watery. A bit thinned out given where we are now. I think it's a bit late in the day for love, don't you?

MARTÓN: But Graydon. There's no logic to it. It's not dependent on. . . . It separates us from the beast I suppose. At the end of the day what else do you get?

(Hilton Lasker enters.)

HILTON: Ah, what a place this is.

MARTÓN: Gray, I have tickets for a weekend for two in Cabo San Lucas. Think about it. Soften, Gray. Soften.

(Martón leaves.)

MASSEY *(By way of explaining):* English men.

HILTON *(Shudders in sympathetic disgust):* Ugh. How's my favorite kid in the world! How's my baby boy that I love! Well? You comin' back into the fold? You movin' back in? Can I call Helen and tell her? She's at the Diet Center being weighed right now I can reach her!

MASSEY: Actually. No. But I do have, for you, a check for the seven hundred and fifty thousand dollars.

HILTON: A check! Gee. That's really something. A check. A check. *You* think I can be bought? You miserable little brat? You think that covers your debt? My daughter is blowing up like a puffer fish and you think money will assuage that? That's not how you pay a debt in this country. You have a hell of a lot to learn!

MASSEY: Hilly. Stop. Really. I'm not going back to Helen, I'm marrying a Stoat on Belgrave Square.

HILTON: I'll have your balls in Hong Kong Harbor and your *kishkas* in the Negev by dinner time.

(Toffler enters. He is dressed. Pale, but not especially weak, though his clothes are too big for him and he has a bandage about the neck.)

MASSEY: Hey. You're meant to be in bed.

TOFFLER: No, I'm really not. I was watching this awful lady on tv . . . something called "A Symposium on Light and Hope." You know? I mean, what is this? She maybe—she does people some good, she must, 'cause they're calling her from their sick beds. And I think she makes them feel a little better.

HILTON: Uh huh.

TOFFLER: Me? Fuck. I wanted to call her up and say "Hey, lady. I can't get there from here, you know?" *(Beat)* "What about ambiguity" . . . what about all the people who die failed and alone and having to face it without a fucking crystal to send a light into your heart. . . . I just started to feel a little. . . . I wanted a burger and a coke . . . *(Beat)* So weird to start to feel better. I wanted to call her and say, "Listen sweetheart, you're nice, but maybe there are no words . . ."

HILTON: The big blond with the broach.

TOFFLER: Yeah. That's her.

HILTON: Yeah. She's cute, and she's probably makin' a bundle, but she's not that smart.

TOFFLER: So the thing is, I'm gonna check out of this charnel house here . . . see what happens . . .

HILTON: Yeah, it's a real pig sty. It's the place that's makin' you sick.

TOFFLER: No. It's not the place, it's him that's making me sick. I don't think you're the world's greatest doctor, pal. Which I'm sure is news to you. Listen, I know I'm sick. I mean, clearly I'm sick. But I think I was misdiagnosed and so does my dad who's a malpractice lawyer and has never lost a case, and who won't take a cent until after I see the first hundred million and we're gonna sue your ass. And so, doctor, fuck you.

MASSEY: You're feeling better aren't you, you ungrateful shit.

TOFFLER: See ya.

MASSEY: For God's sake, Jonathon, you must let me help you. I can help you. Please, I implore you.

TOFFLER: Gray, you're a con artist and I'm not going to be some sort of pathetic, little, dying, moral test case, not for myself and certainly not for you. You gotta let me go, Gray. You gotta let me go. *(Beat)* By the way, we met once before. I came to you in Beverly Hills three years ago, and you told me I had no problems.

(Toffler exits.)

MASSEY *(Staring icily at Hilton):* I own Panno-Anglo-Suez-Oceanic. I am a general partner in Fiasco Films. And that means you work for me. So you're going to do just as your told. Let's go on. Let's go on making money. Let's be decent to one another. Hilly. You're so smart. You're going to be a great man. Let me help you. As for Helen. Soon there'll be . . . an opening at Fiasco. You can help me replace the current . . . studio head and we'll put in Helen. Let's look out at the world together. And make it ours.

(Silence.)

HILTON: You know. You've finally arrived. Welcome to America. Boss. Feels good, doesn't it?

Scene Six

The stage becomes a gallery in the Los Angeles Museum of Art. The walls lined with George Stubbs paintings. It is night. The rest of the cast is there in black tie and formal gowns.

HELEN: Do they validate parking here, or what, 'cause I'm . . .
TELLMAN: I'm really not sure. Jet lag. Canape?
HELEN: No, they've got dairy. I'm lactose intolerant.
JOCELYN: This grotesque heat. God, how do they stay awake in it? It's February for God's sake.
STOAT *(To Tellman, hissing)* Tellman, inform the curator that my husband insists the lighting be lower.
HILTON: You must be the mother. Isn't he something?
JOCELYN: Well, we're very proud.
HELEN *(To Swifty, overlapping):* Ah, Lord Kitterson!
SWIFTY: Dear girl . . . I adored your last picture.
HELEN: Oh thanks. It's a Fiasco.
SWIFTY: Let's be sure that these fiascos keep making a profit for us, my dear.
TELLMAN: Canape, madame?
BRACKETT: Thanks.
HELEN: You know I'm not so crazy about these paintings anymore, dad. They don't hold up do they?
HILTON: Look, they like it kid. It's art. Don't ask me.
BRACKETT: So many Stubbs! So many! Oh . . . *(To Stoat)* You must be so proud of your husband!
STOAT: Oh yes, we all are. How could we not be? Look at what he's done.
JOCELYN: Ah, Mr. Lasker. We enjoyed the basket of kiwi you sent over to the hotel.

HILTON: My pleasure.

JOCELYN: However, your deposit in Lucerne was just a wee bit light this week.

HILTON: Oy!

(Helen stops Tellman with his hors d'oeuvres tray. She drips some liquid from a vial onto an hors d'oeuvre. Massey enters in black tie. There is applause.)

HELEN *(To Tellman):* Sweetie, sweetie make sure the new wife gets this particular anchovy. *(Beat)* Graydon, Graydon.

MASSEY: Not now, Helen.

STOAT: You look marvelous, darling.

MASSEY: We just got a fax from the Koreans, my little Stoatette, they're in for three hundred.

STOAT: Only three?

SWIFTY: Joc, Graydon just informed me that Lisbon is in for six.

JOCELYN: Six! Six is not enough. He told me they'd go as high as twelve. Not good enough, Gray.

MASSEY: Ladies and gentlemen, it gives me great pleasure to open the Massey wing for British Art here at the Los Angeles Museum of Art. A place that symbolizes internationalism—a place of connection.

(Toffler enters, unnoticed, also in black tie. He is so pale as to appear apparition-like; the white bandage still around his neck. Massey catches his eye and goes on with his speech.)

Where two great cultures can celebrate the marriage between them—and our great achievements. Not just the Massey wing here, but also our work in rebuilding the San Pedro clinic as one of the great, great onocolgy centers on the Pacific rim for which we need another forty million right now.

HILTON: I'm in for five.

MASSEY: Fabulous, and oh I see Hal and Jerry in for ten, and Sybill and Ed, ever generous, in for twenty-five. We got it! The Massey Foundation thanks you. Because we all of us—under this sky—are connected to one another—we don't live alone—on the rocks—we are linked. And we all have to give. Because if you don't give—at the end of the day—you're nothing. *(Beat)* Let this gallery symbolize our strength and our fragility—so magnificently rendered by George Stubbs—and let us see in these paintings—the frailness of our endeavors and their importance as well . . . *(He smiles)* We have champagne and beluga, please. More than anything else I can say, I implore you—tonight—*(Beat)* Enjoy yourselves. Enjoy yourselves. Enjoy yourselves.

(There is applause. Hilton comes up to Massey.)

HILTON: That was great, boss.

MASSEY *(Quiet):* Did you put the bomb in my mother's trunk?

HILTON *(A whisper):* I got rid of that little English fruit, didn't I? It's done.

HELEN *(To Tellman, who is passing out champagne):* You know . . . if he was born in this country, they could run him for president.

BRACKETT: Doctor. The painting you gave me! It's on the wall.

MASSEY: Yes. It's a fake, my darling. You needn't worry. You got the real one. Most of these are fakes.

STOAT: Oh, thank you. I adore anchovies.

MASSEY *(To all):* Enjoy!

(Massey hugs Helen. The lights go down on everyone but Massey and Toffler, who are illuminated for a moment. Massey looks at Toffler. Blackout.)